AN
HONORABLE
EXIT

AN
HONORABLE
EXIT

ÉRIC VUILLARD

Translated from the French
by Mark Polizzotti

OTHER PRESS
New York

Production editor: Yvonne E. Cárdenas
Text designer: Cassandra J. Pappas
This book was set in Adobe Caslon Pro and Alternate Gothic
by Alpha Design & Composition of Pittsfield NH

1 3 5 7 9 10 8 6 4 2

Library of Congress Cataloging-in-Publication Data
Names: Vuillard, Éric, author. | Polizzotti, Mark, translator.
Title: An honorable exit / Éric Vuillard ; translated from the
French by Mark Polizzotti.
Other titles: Sortie honorable. English
Description: New York : Other Press, 2023.
Identifiers: LCCN 2022044629 (print) | LCCN 2022044630 (ebook) |
ISBN 9781635423525 (hardcover) | ISBN 9781635423532 (ebook)
Subjects: LCSH: Indochinese War, 1946-1954—Fiction. | Indochina—
History—1945-—Fiction. | LCGFT: Historical fiction.
Classification: LCC PQ2682.U45 S6713 2023 (print) |
LCC PQ2682.U45 (ebook) | DDC 843/.914—dc23/eng/20221122
LC record available at https://lccn.loc.gov/2022044629
LC ebook record available at https://lccn.loc.gov/2022044630

for Stéphane Tiné †

Top Secret Addendum
to a Report on the Labor Inspection

One must travel," wrote Montaigne. "Travel makes one modest," Flaubert added. And Taine took it up a notch: "We travel for a change, not of place, but of ideas." But what if the opposite were true? In a travel guide to Indochina from 1923, after a page advertising the firm of Ridet & Co., a gunsmith located in the center of Hanoi providing "weapons and munitions for hunting and warfare, all accessories for hunters and tourists, automatic pistols or rifles" (this before any mention of "picturesque Upper Tonkin, abounding in natural curiosities"), we come across a brief dictionary, a conversation manual for vacationers, of which the first rudiments are: "Go find me a rickshaw, go quickly, go quietly, turn right, turn left, turn back, put up the top, put down the top, wait for me a moment, take me to the bank, to the jeweler's, to the café, to the police station, to the dealership." This was the basic vocabulary for a French tourist in Indochina.

On June 25, 1928, at the crack of dawn, three austere figures set out from Saigon on a short journey. A wisp of fog hung over the buildings. The car drove quickly. Even with the top up, it was chilly out, and before long the front-seat passenger wrapped himself in a blanket. As it happened, Tholance, Delamarre, and their secretary were hardly your average travelers; they formed the kernel of a new colonial administration and were the very first labor inspectors appointed to French Indochina. Suspicions of ill treatment at a Michelin plantation had made a lot of noise, and after a revolt by the workers they had been assigned to ensure that the paltry regulations serving as a labor code were being followed, ostensibly for the Vietnamese coolies' protection. Soon the car left the city outskirts for rows of thatched huts. The landscape was beautiful, of an almost aggressive green. The river overspilled its banks, and behind a narrow strip of land you could glimpse a multitude of small, sparkling patches of water.

Finally, the path plunged into the forest, and the travelers felt both a kind of enchantment and a vague anxiety. On each side of the road was an immobile parade, implacably repeated. They entered an immense forest. But this was no typical forest: neither a wild, overgrown tropical rainforest nor the dark, dense forest of dreams where children get lost. No, this forest was stranger still, perhaps even wilder, and darker. Entering it, the travelers shuddered. It seemed that in this forest, by a curious sorcery, all the trees grew at exactly the same distance from one another. One tree, then another tree, then another and another, as if the forest were composed of a single specimen multiplied ad infinitum.

At night, in the cold hours, men pace steadily from tree to tree, gripping small knives. It takes them five seconds to go several short steps; then they bend down, straighten up, and leave a gash in the tree's bark: these efforts take a maximum of fifteen seconds. And so, more or less every twenty seconds, each man reaches another tree, and in the next row another man follows him, and over hundreds and hundreds of meters, hundreds of men advance, barefoot and in canvas trousers, lantern in one hand and knife in the other, and slice the bark. Then the tree slowly begins to drip. It looks like milk. But it's not milk, it's latex. And every night, each man bleeds roughly eighteen hundred trees; eighteen hundred times the man takes his knife to the bark, eighteen hundred times he makes a notch, cutting off a fine strip about two milli-meters thick, eighteen hundred times he must be careful not to touch the heartwood. And as our inspectors cross through the endless plantation in their car, even as they admire how Taylor and Michelin have managed to ward off "the natural idleness" of the Annamite workers via rationally organized labor; even as they stare transfixed at the glacial immensity of the work, marveling at the extent to which this forest, the pitiless organization of this forest, represents an unprecedented struggle against wasted time, they experience a kind of terror.

But even the best regulated system has its failures. And at nine o'clock that morning, about twenty kilometers before their arrival at the plantation office, Labor Inspector Emile Delamarre noticed three young Tonkinese by the side of the road. He was unfortunate enough to lean out, and saw that they were bound together with iron wire. It must have seemed odd to him, incongruous, these three shoeless men tied together, and so he immediately ordered his driver to stop.

The three men were filthy, dressed in rags; they were under a foreman's supervision. Delamarre got out of the car a little groggily, stumbled in the mud, and advanced with difficulty toward the prisoners. Once he'd reached them, he looked for a moment at the foreman, who, at the sight of Delamarre's expensive suit, doffed his hat.

The air was already warm and humid. Delamarre noticed that the prisoners were covered in scabies. At a glance, he saw that the metal wire was digging into their wrists, and he decided to question them directly, in Vietnamese. After a banal exchange of words and some hesitation, one of them said he had tried to escape. He was what they called a *deserter*: he had run away from the plantation under cover of darkness but had just been recaptured. Delamarre no doubt found the punishment disproportionate, but it wasn't really his purview. He contented himself with a curt remark to the foreman, then turned around, scraped his soles on the roadside, and got back into the car. "To the plantation," he ordered.

During the rest of the trip, he tried to forget that painful scene, and thank God, when they arrived at the plantation they were treated to a warm welcome. After a cursory glimpse of the facilities, they were introduced to the director of the Michelin establishments in Cochinchina, Monsieur Alpha, accompanied by the plantation manager, Monsieur Traiaire, and several European employees. The group of them made a more extensive tour: the coolie housing, tiny garden plots, showers, infirmary, quartermaster's stores, water tower. The inspectors viewed the new equipment with admiration. As they emerged from the structures, Delamarre, seizing on a moment alone with the director, inquired about the stocks he'd noticed at the beginning of their visit, near the housing. Monsieur Alpha looked uncomfortably surprised; he turned to his aide, Monsieur Triaire, and asked for an explanation.

"I built that for deserters," Triaire said, a bit sheepishly. "We don't keep them longer than one night, and only attached by one foot!"

"Are there other stocks on the plantation?" Delamarre asked.

"Not a one," Triaire answered, categorically.

The visit continued. Now they were at the kitchens; they were to get a complete tour of the premises. Triaire began by vaunting the modern layout, the cleanliness. Suddenly, as they passed a closed door, Delamarre asked what was behind it. The other man answered with a shrug, probably a closet, he didn't have the keys. As Delamarre insisted on entering, Triaire went off to find them. Finally, the supervisor returned, breathless, and opened the door. The room was empty of people, but at the back were stocks with nine foot-holes.

The director turned sharply to Triaire and demanded an explanation. Triaire stammered; the director raised his voice. But, just as in the theater a little farce is played out in the foreground that is contradicted by something in the background, they suddenly heard moans coming from the adjacent room. Again the door was locked, again they'd have to fetch the keys. On the strength of his authority, the labor inspector furiously ordered them to break the door down. And lo and behold, it suddenly opened, they had miraculously found the keys, what a scatterbrain that Triaire is! But instead of defusing the situation, this strange blunder only heightened an obscure fear that had slowly been permeating the labor inspectors. And as the door opens—they can feel it fully now—and the moans grow louder, they enter another world.

A man is lying on his back, spent, exhausted, both feet bound, half-naked. The man is writhing on the floor, trying desperately to cover his genitals with a filthy rag that he clutches against him as best he can. Then, as the small group stands there, stunned by what they have just discovered, Triaire rushes up and, ripping away the rag that the poor man was holding to his trembling, emaciated body, cries: "Let's hope he hasn't hurt himself!" The remark is incongruous, and the labor inspector doesn't immediately understand what he meant. Is Triaire suggesting that the man has been bound like this *for his own good*?

The coolie was now almost naked, for all to see. It was a horrific scene. They freed him from his shackles, stood him up, and the guards roughly examined every inch of his body, as if the man had tried to kill himself or was concealing something. The room was poorly lit, sordid. The man was atrociously thin. He could barely stand. He was terrified.

The director reprimanded Triaire. "What the hell is going on here!" he cried. "I don't know, sir," Triaire repeated over and over, shouting in turn at a guard to fetch an orderly *now*. They had to wait. The wait was endless. The Vietnamese man was skeletal, moribund, forced to remain standing amid the directors and the two strangers whose language he didn't speak. He swayed, and the Frenchmen fell silent. Now and then, a drop of rain fell heavily on the sheet metal roof. A gust of cool air blew through the room. And Triaire repeated as if to himself, "I don't understand."

Finally the orderly arrived. Perhaps he thought to reassure the inspectors by stating that he was "treating a dysentery case." But this surprising declaration only made the atmosphere more tense. Delamarre thought, "And this is how you cure him, by chaining him half-naked to a post?" He ordered in a cold voice, "Strip this man down completely!" Triaire made a sign to the two guards, the coolie recoiled in fear, but he was too weak to resist. They removed his undershirt. The man was now entirely naked, as we will be one day before our judges. He stood with his head bowed; he looked dead. Inspector Delamarre approached the man slowly, very slowly, and walked around him. He motioned for his colleague to come closer: "I would like you to note that this man's back bears distinct traces of six cane blows."

The next day, Delamarre went to the other Michelin plantation, where several suicides by hanging had recently been reported. The Michelin firm was wondering about "the reasons for this *epidemic of suicides*," as the labor inspector's report put it. From the list he'd been given, these suicides had occurred with alarming frequency. Pham-thi-Nhi, by hanging on May 19; Pham-van-Ap, by hanging on May 21; Ta-dinh-Tri, by hanging the same day; Lê-ba-Hanh, by hanging on the 24th; Dô-thê-Tuât, by hanging on June 10; Nguyên-Sang, by hanging on June 13; Tran-Cuc, by hanging that very morning. In all, seven suicides in one month.

During his tour, the inspector discovers deep contusions on the coolies; and when he questions them, out comes a flood of stories of humiliation and terror; and despite the denials, Delamarre comes upon a whole bundle of canes in a closet; and as usual, the plantation director knows nothing about it; and as usual, he seems very afflicted, declares that if only he'd known about certain excesses, if only he'd put a stop to them sooner by transferring an overly zealous young assistant, he could never have imagined such outbursts; and as usual, the director expresses his profound regret; and as usual, these abuses are chalked up to exceptions, blunders, the cruelty of a guard, the sadism of a subaltern. The inspector draws up a scrupulous report, and the administration formulates a few recommendations. They result in not one single reform or indictment. That year, the Michelin firm realizes a record profit of 93 million francs.

Several years earlier, André Michelin had made the acquaintance of Frederick Winslow Taylor on the occasion of a luncheon held in the latter's honor at the Prunier restaurant in Paris. Over dessert, Taylor, who according to Michelin's account was "modesty itself," had shyly spelled out for them the basic tenets of his method. But to better understand André Michelin's admiration for Taylor's theories; to truly experience the dread the labor inspectors felt as their car rolled at daybreak past that geometric forest, where all the trees were planted at equal intervals so that each coolie could always take the same number of steps at the same cadence; to fully grasp what is meant by "Taylor's modesty," the quality Michelin saw in him, let us quote this small excerpt from Frederick W. Taylor's *Shop Management*, in which he debuted his "principles of scientific management": "A man with only the intelligence of an average laborer can be taught to do the most difficult and delicate work if it is repeated enough times; and his lower mental caliber renders him more fit than the mechanic to stand the monotony of repetition."

Thus, according to Taylor, Pham-thi-Nhi, ID number 2762, who hanged himself on May 19, 1928, at the plantation at Dau-tieng, was nothing other than a *man with only the intelligence of an average laborer taught to do the most repetitive work*; it appears, however, that despite his *lower mental caliber*, he couldn't abide the *monotony of repetition*. And Pham-van-Ap, ID number 1309, who hanged himself on May 21, 1928, was also nothing other than a *man with only the intelligence of an average laborer taught to do the most repetitive work*; and yet he, too, was apparently unable to withstand the *monotony of repetition*.

That same year, 30 percent of the workmen died on the plantation, more than three hundred people. Delamarre again saw the thin wrists, gashed by iron wire, of the three haggard captives, those *deserters* with vacant eyes whom he had encountered at dawn. He felt ashamed. The truth was there, plain as day. What difference did their miserable labor contract make, when it could be used to coerce them like that? Getting back on the road that evening, Inspector Delamarre understood that by running away from the plantation, these men were only trying to save their skins.

Dupont of the Lodges

The Tonkin region in the north of Vietnam abounds in extraordinary hilly landscapes, which travel writers refer to as "dreamscapes." The steep cliffs, limpid lakes, and prodigious waterfalls seem to come straight out of a Chinese painting. It's as if they've been painted with a worn-down brush, so that the minimal lines suggest only a misty frontier. But by September 1950, the military outpost from which the French had been admiring these sublime landscapes for a quarter century was receiving provisions only by air, leaving it dangerously isolated. It was tricky getting hold of air-dropped supplies, and they were beginning to worry about having enough food. The situation was growing dire. The plantations had been deserted by large contingents of workers, who had joined the rebellion. The French were now facing a veritable army. And so, after much hesitation, the French general staff resigned itself to evacuating the position. Too late. The very day the evacuation order was sent, the

Vietminh launched a blistering attack. The French immediately parachuted in legionnaires as reinforcements, but the assault was so swift and lethal that they didn't even have time to intervene, and the post fell.

From one bloody misadventure to the next, from order to ill-advised counterorder, the regiment that had evacuated from Cao Bang advanced painstakingly through the jungle. It finally managed to reach a second column. But by nightfall, their situation becoming ever more alarming, attacked from all sides, the survivors attempted a desperate retreat. The enemy gave them no quarter, and after many fierce clashes, the two columns were annihilated.

Some ten days later, on Thursday, October 19, 1950, at the National Assembly in Paris, Edouard Herriot, presiding, addressed a formulaic homage to *our* armed forces, *our* heroic soldiers; he then evoked their struggle in Indochina with great dignity. He even deemed it appropriate to add that their mission was "to ensure the independence of a nation associated with our country in the context of the French Union." He cast a circular glance around the chamber. The benches were full. Once he had duly expressed *our* deep condolences to the grieving families, he quickly moved on and ceded the floor to the first interpellator, Mr. Juge.

In the name of the Communist delegation, the deputy asked how the government intended to respond to Ho Chi Minh's offer of an exchange of prisoners. His speech lasted several minutes, the other deputies began to yawn—it was so unseasonably warm that October! Ties were loosened, belts undone by a notch. Finally, fifteen minutes later, another deputy, Frédéric-Dupont, took the floor, and immediately the benches woke up. It's just that Frédéric-Dupont was not your usual parliamentarian, but a deputy-capital-D, with loud opinions. To do him justice, we should add that a considerable share of his reputation came from his fervent interest in the concierges of apartment buildings. They say he introduced dozens and dozens of bills aimed at improving their meager living conditions—hence his nickname, "Dupont of the Lodges."

It is profoundly moving to note such fidelity to an unjustly despised guild, to those passive, hardworking witnesses to our lives, who sort our mail, bar unwanted visitors, and take out our trash. But to better understand our deputy's commitment to them, we must go back to the criteria of their recruitment. For this, we have to linger a moment on the life of Jean Chiappe, the famous police commissioner, one of the founders of modern policing. An assiduous reader of the right-wing rags *Le Gringoire* and *L'Action française*, Chiappe especially admired the reactionary polemical writer Charles Maurras. In the evening, his back pressed against a hot water bottle, constipated, he feverishly leafed through the master's pamphlets and political diatribes, hoping against hope that from them would spring the energetic regime that could redeem France. When he was in a good mood—say, after a propitious haul or the successful repression of a strike—he sighed beneath his bedside lamp over the weft of imaginary loves that Maurras spun in his *provincial reveries*. But Jean Chiappe's true passion was his job. A zealot, he filled the ranks of peacekeepers with as many toughs, thugs, and agitators as possible, in order to have a police force that was battle-hardened, accommodating, and narrow-minded. To improve the daily lot of his shock troops, he helped get their wives jobs as concierges, to fatten the kitty. And besides, you can never have enough information about unkempt tenants or unstable petty landlords; it was therefore judicious to stuff the concierge lodges of Paris with reliable individuals. We now understand better why Frédéric-Dupont, who fell in line with Chiappe's convictions, would tirelessly support the concierges: he was actually supporting a veritable army of poll workers, missionaries, touts, barroom propagandists—and more than anything, he was boosting a diligent, effective clientele, the spouses of his peacekeepers, an armada of informants.

Frédéric-Dupont was therefore not merely the extravagant legendary deputy, the excessive and whimsical maniac that his former colleagues describe. And so, while Frédéric-Dupont studiously walks down the aisle that October 19, 1950, shaking a few hands and uttering a few pleasantries along the way, let's unspool his long career for a closer look. Let's pick up the book lying on his bedside table and quickly leaf through the minor novel of his existence.

Edouard Frédéric-Dupont was born in the seventh arrondissement of Paris and was a true native of the neighborhood, speaking its lingo, knowing its codes, wearing its livery. He had an odd kisser, did Dupont, though to be fair, he received a head wound while marching in the fascist riots of February 1934, and maybe that accounted for his unpleasant moon face. But the residents of the seventh arrondissement recompensed him for that war wound, constantly electing and reelecting him with something like 95 percent of the vote, veritable plebiscites. A devotee of General Franco, he later voted to grant Marshal Pétain full powers. In 1941 he became vice president of the Council of Paris, but feeling the wind change, he then refused to support the proposed budget for 1944. Finally, he resigned from the Council, mere moments before its collapse. Several months later, France was liberated. This act of bravery earned him in extremis the Medallion of the Resistance and the Legion of Honor.

But let's move on now and leap over a few hedges! To recap his prodigious career: sixty-two years as an elected official in Paris (a record), thirteen tenures as deputy, more than forty years of parliamentary life; he served under three republics and was a member of ten political parties, ultimately running as a Front National candidate alongside Olivier d'Ormesson. But more than anything, "Dupont of the chatterboxes," as they affectionately called him in the backrooms, was a great *champion of reforms*. Among his most notable achievements, he was involved in the creation of the Paris beltway, the building of a parking lot, and the restoration of the Invalides gardens. A stellar record.

But on that October 19, 1950, Frédéric-Dupont is at one of the summits of his career; the war in Indochina has put him front and center. He is a one-man preservation society for the empire and the advocate of our army. A flatus of luminescence wafts from the skylight, the scribes discreetly take turns near the podium. Dupont hitches up his britches (plus sizes sure aren't what they used to be), does up the second button of his jacket (of a cut that flatters his embonpoint), making sure it isn't wrinkled, and clears his throat. Frédéric-Dupont grips the podium. The benches are filled, the balconies filling, his buddies urging him on. With a pensive hand, he mops his scalp, mustering his few remaining hairs, and launches into his grand diatribe.

First, with a devastated gesture, he evokes "the tragedy of Cao Bang" and deplores "the material and moral abandonment in which our heroic expeditionary corps was left." Scattered laughter breaks out. The secretaries note that quips are coming from all sides. The lights are bright. Dupont feels a vague distress. On the governmental benches, the ministers are fidgeting. In his telling, the army in Indochina is short of everything; and stabbing an accusatory finger toward the secretary of the armed forces, Dupont shouts, anguished and scarlet in the face, that they even had to replace their barbed wire with bamboo spikes!

Max Brusset: "This is an outrage!"

Max Brusset's retort is memorable. And, like everything having to do with memory, it originates in a slow sedimentation. For him to effectively shout "This is an outrage!" in just the right circumstances required several generations of notables. From Max Brusset's goiter, the expression takes root in the gorge of his grandfather

Jean-Baptiste, a senator and the president of the notaries of the Haute-Saône, a marvelous function. Max, for his part, was a member of the honorary committee and the steering committee of the *Revue des Deux Mondes*, which has always been generous. He was also an owner of Radio Méditerranée, then CEO of Satas, a company that made postage meter machines, of a patented model endowed with an exclusive and revolutionary process named after the wild boar. But then we see him as an adviser to the national electric company, then to L'Oréal, then to Henkel-France, which produced adhesives and detergent. He's a flexible guy, Max; with his pleasant radio face, he adapts, moving from radio waves to postage stamps; from stamps to the distribution of electricity; and from electricity, which brightens life, to cosmetics, which are accessory to it; and from cosmetics, which beautify, to detergents, which corrode.

His wife, Marie, was a Vallery-Radot, the pride of the bourgeoisie. In the sixteenth century, the Radots were merchants, handing down a modest coffer and clipboard from father to son. A century later, they were top surgeons; another century later, they became royal notaries. And off they went. In the nineteenth century, Lazare-André Radot settled in Avallon as a lawyer. His son,

Vincent Félix Vallery-Radot, went up to Paris and had a
prodigious career. From the Royal Library of the Louvre,
he hoisted himself to the office of Minister of Agricul-
ture and Commerce under the Second Empire. He was
a jack of all trades, that Vincent Félix, writing articles,
publishing books, and finally making off with the Legion
of Honor. But more than anything, Vincent Félix married. And here again, he was crafty and ambitious: he
married the granddaughter of Dr. Jean-Joseph Sue, and
through her, he simultaneously married into the Academy of Medicine, into literature, and into History with a
capital H, garnishing his family tree with Louis Pasteur
and Eugène Sue, with a steward to the duc d'Orléans
and a member of the French Academy. And this continued with René Vallery-Radot, man of letters, collabora-
tor, also on the *Revue des Deux Mondes*; and then again
with Louis Pasteur Vallery-Radot, who straddled both
academies, French and Medical. What a tribe, those
Vallery-Radots! And in fact, it was the distillation of
that lineage, a florilegium of the French bourgeoisie, that
was actually coming out of Max Brusset's mouth that
October 19, 1950, at the National Assembly at around
10 a.m. And while Little Max, the kid from Neufchâ-
teau, retreats deep into his suit, behind his brown tie and
too-white collar, while in the back of the shop (aka, *his
soul*) he gnaws on who knows what pathological fright,

deathly pale and gnarring covert, sad, venomous words that he quietly mutters to himself, not hearing them, perhaps not even thinking; while Little Max, timid, gaze unfixed, shrivels into himself, the Max who is a deputy from Charente-Maritime raises his arm passionately and opens his trap wide. At that, his entire genealogy of notables, the *grand* Brussets, send the *little* Brussets of the past packing; and his in-laws, the bonzes of the *Revue des Deux Mondes*, the manitous of the surgical and notarial trades, rise in turn, and like a symbol of national representation, crystallizing the will of thousands into one, all the Radots, Brussets, and Vallerys bray like a single individual: "This is an outrage!"

But Max Brusset is not content with that admirable interjection. One hour later, he again flaps his gums to say: "Alas, we got ours!" And shortly after that, this piquant retort: "It's his master's voice!" evoking the Algerian populace. Then a good half hour passes, during which he scratches his balls under the desk, and after a quick nap, jerked out of his slumbers by the fierceness of the debates, he tosses out to the round his most celebrated quip: "Are they handing out awards?" But at the end of the day, he'll have one more retort, a moral dictum that says it all. Red in the face, breathing hard, he hoists himself up on his pins and utters in a deathly, bloodless voice: "Mr. President, you seem to have more regard for Mr. Tillon than for Mr. Capitant." Which in plain French means: "You have more regard for a Communist than for a member of the Rally for France." Which in old French means: "You have more regard for a former metalworker than for a professor at the Paris law school!" Which in the French of Molière means: "You have more regard for a country bumpkin than for one of our own!"

Interlude

═══

Finally, at around noon, after several memorable interventions, Assembly President Edouard Herriot emerged from his prodigious indolence, shook his enormous girth, and declared that the rest of the debate was to be adjourned until the next public session, in two hours. It was twelve-fifteen and the president buttoned his jacket, as businessmen and politicians habitually do by a kind of conditioned reflex. Workers, postal employees, railwaymen, and crane operators never button their jackets; they stuff their hands in their pockets or plant them on their hips, letting the wings of their smocks cover their elbows. But businessmen and politicians have always had a problem with bulges, with the paunch. Age is part of it; but salaries, perks, and gratuities are the main cause of that deformity.

Immediately the benches emptied out. Herriot and a few colleagues went off to lunch at Rollet, on Rue de Bourgogne. And as they maneuvered around the old master, they commented on Pierre Cot's intervention later that morning, which set the Assembly on its ear. "Is it true," one of them asked, "that the war is costing us a billion a day?" A member of the Finance Committee, who trotted along in the gutter so as to leave the sidewalk free for the president, confirmed: "We are indeed spending a billion francs a day on this war, according to the Finance Minister's reports. That is the official figure." At the evocation of this figure, the Assembly benches had started to grumble. A billion. That's kind of a lot. Embarrassed looks passed between the rows; they gulped, did spit-takes, compared notes. It did seem pretty huge. A billion a day. There's never enough for allocations or financial aid; all sorts of welfare initiatives have to wait their turn in the name of fiscal realism. They tell us, finger pointed upward, that if we spend more than we can repay, well then, that's the road to bankruptcy. And the old foxes who spend their lives with their snouts hovering over the slightest decimal, who skimp on a penny here and a penny there, those fierce guardians of our small change—suddenly, for such an exorbitant, vain, murderous expenditure, they don't hesitate, hands on hearts and bawling the national anthem, to throw a billion out the window every single day.

By now, the restaurant is in sight. The shadow of President Herriot advances on the sidewalk with its formidable limp, leaning his vast corpulence on his cane, filled with nebulosities and obscurities, twisted, stumbling along, waddling like certain turkeys, his tongue worrying an aching tooth, or perhaps some loose bridgework. Finally, once inside the restaurant, after several Pantagruelian torsions of the torso, once his gargantuan pot has settled into the cove of his armchair, the old bison ruminates.

They start by ordering a glass of Kessler, then pause a moment to admire its lemon-yellow hue with palish-green tints, in the wan light that struggles to filter through the meager windows of the dining room. President Herriot, who had been exasperated by that Prudhommesque session, brings the glass to his nostrils and tries desperately to appreciate the preserved scents, the accents of citrus, quince, plum—no go: his bad mood is stronger than treats, exasperation wins out over the pleasures of the table, and he slugs down his twenty-franc drink as if it were cheap rotgut. The waiter recommends the terrine of foie gras in port aspic, or perhaps the veal piccata, nicely topped with capers, which marry beautifully with the equilibrium of that rich, mellow wine. But Herriot doesn't give a shit; with an annoyed wave of the hand, he orders the terrine just to get rid of the fellow, and he reserves for dessert a chocolate éclair before they can all be gobbled by his colleagues, as happened last week! The waiter retreats with a smile. Herriot has a stomachache and loosens his belt under the table; he's already seventy-eight, Old Herriot, making it forty-six years that he's been shuffling his gaiters through the benches of councils and assemblies, and he's fed up. He smiles vaguely at his tablemates, the youngest of whom comment on their colleagues' diatribes and restage the Battle of Cao Bang with napkins and forks. But Herriot doesn't give a flyer about Cao Bang. He takes out his legendary pipe, roguish eye at the summit of a mountain of fat, then doles out a few all-purpose phrases in a municipal tone, for above all he is Mayor of Lyon, alderman, and will continue to be for seven more years; all in all, almost half a century. For thirty-five years before the Second World War, and eleven years, ten months, and eight days after it, he has watched over Lyon, over the little grocers of Saint-Jean and the minor annuitants of the Presqu'île.

Paraphrasing the separation of Church and State, they say that in Herriot, there was a separation of brain and stomach, separation of municipal spirit and municipal carcass. And while he handed down many sound and discriminating judgments during his long career, he also thundered quite a few stupidities from the bench. Such as when, during the debates around the birth of the French Union, he pompously declared: "If we granted equal rights to our colonized populations, we would become the colony of our colonies."

It's hard for us to imagine what it means to be mayor of Lyon for so many years. It's hard to imagine what it presupposes in municipal dealings, municipal hand-shakes, in skill, finesse, wiles, backstabbery. It's hard to imagine the number of bodies a guy like Edouard Herriot left in his wake, how many corpses, how many colleagues executed and careers throttled, for this one fat slob to climb the steps of the Lyon city hall and install himself on the throne for half a century.

The deputies in his entourage were still trading remarks about the session, mocking this one and that one, bringing up Cao Bang, "the tragic events," "the situation in Indochina"; they parroted the previous evening's newspaper. Thank goodness, that's when the terrine arrived. Herriot leapt on it with his little butter knife and thick, fur-covered paw. He scooped up half, no one batted an eye. His face was tired; for a moment, his eyes looked vacant, his breathing was labored. No doubt there wasn't much Edouard Herriot left in that huge carcass. There was the cacique, the sachem of the Rhone. The rest was dead.

Dupont of the Lodges entered the room and headed toward the next table, greeting President Herriot in passing. That noon, in the mounting hubbub, Herriot was suddenly no more than a tired old man, floating in the void. But the beast continued to live and feed itself. It knew that when it entered a room, the crowd got to its feet. It knew that the young beasts, who were just waiting for it to die, circled around it in silence, but that when it finished speaking and gave out a little burp, everyone again stood and applauded. It knew that streets would be named after it. It knew they would pronounce a funeral oration for it. It knew that the applause, the stiff hellos, the bowing and scraping, were already the start of its funeral oration. From his place at the head of the table, barely lifting his enormous eyelids, Herriot wiped his lips and chin with a numb gesture. His public life was now no more than a sovereign routine.

The Grand Coalition

═══

Slowly, the deputies returned from lunch and got back in session. The public retook their seats in the spectator boxes. "Shh! Come this way!" murmured the usher, with a hand motion. "Come this way!" As if in school, people found places in the back row. One fellow explained, "Look over there, it's President Herriot! You know, the Mayor of Lyon…" "I recognize him!" an old woman blurted. "He looks older than in his photos…" In the amphitheater, a swarthy gentleman took the floor, an Arab. "Is he a deputy?" a young woman asked in astonishment. "I think so," answered her husband.

The Arab is a Kabyle, and he is indeed a deputy. His name is Abderrahmane-Chérif Djemad. He's a Communist deputy from Constantine. A peasant's son who had emigrated to France, after some brief studies he had been a mason and a roadworker. "How many more Algerians, how many more Moroccans, how many more colonials will be felled by this horrible fate?" he thunders, referring to the infantrymen who, in Indochina, in fact make up the bulk of *our army*. His vehemence seems misplaced in this nearly empty room.

The distant faces of the few colleagues present seem to float before him, and the deputy from Constantine feels weary. He sits back down, throat constricted. What's the use of speaking here, when all the speeches run into one another like paths in a labyrinth? Nothing remains.

Now the rows were filling up again. People chatted. His colleagues returned from the canteen, the way a camarilla of guests passes imperceptibly from the dining room to the salon. Abderrahmane-Chérif Djemad felt a fine layer of resentment settle over him, and it made him sad.

There was a flurry in the benches: the Socialist group had gotten together for a last-minute huddle, calling to each other in whispers. The session president seemed lost in thought. Suddenly Daniel Mayer rose from his seat, firmly rebuttoned his jacket, and then, in a dignified and measured tone, he declared in the name of the Socialist group that "the Assembly should be unanimous in saluting and honoring the dead, all the dead"; and in response to Djemad's anguished question, he stressed: "without exception." He then rendered "a *tribute to the courage and endurance* of the *soldiers fighting there for France.*" The light is pale. The government representatives suddenly look old, horribly old. Mayer's little couplet is a model of the genre, and it has acted as a wakeup call. It has allowed the members of the grand coalition to immediately bond together. At its signal, they demand everyone's total allegiance: in other words, all those who claim to participate in decision-making, in the government, who aspire to high office, must demonstrate, by their prolonged applause and their unequivocal approbation, in the name of their faction, in the name of Parliament, in the name of social order, that they agree to censure themselves. They must show that in the name of supposedly honorable values such as patriotism, and concealing other interests that are nonetheless the unwritten preamble to any constitution; that in the face of Abderrahmane-Chérif Djemad's disagreeable insinuations and of the nonetheless undeniable fate of the infantrymen, the deputies will mute their differences. Hearing words like *tribute, courage, soldiers*, they all understand immediately, and without further ado, that it's time to dissolve their freedom of speech in a nebulous gobbledygook. Daniel Mayer is rather pleased with the effect he's produced. The applause from left, right, and center confirm that his call was clearly heard, and that his tribute to the soldiers has been carried unanimously. Abderrahmane-Chérif

Djemad's infantrymen are now but a distant memory. It would almost be dizzying, if these weren't real deaths, real corpses.

Finally, once Mayer has sat back down, once he has chewed, swallowed, and spat back his pen cap a couple of times, a broad, familiar silhouette slowly climbs to the podium. "Mr. Mendès France now has the floor."

A Deputy

═══

Throat-clearing on all sides, benches creak, leather squeaks beneath hindquarters settling in, and the speaker sets before him his raft of dead leaves. "Today," he says, "speaking on my own behalf, I would like to state that in my opinion, it has become dangerous to hide the truth from this country." When he heard the word "truth," the Council president, René Pleven, straightened up in silent disapproval. In the corridors, they ran to round up more comrades, muster the troops. Exclamations sounded for a moment throughout the room, but silence was soon restored. And Mendès resumed speaking.

He began by saying that to realize our objectives in Indochina by means of military force, we would first have to win some decisive victories. His gentle but determined gaze swept over the room; no one flinched. Mendès had the gift of following the deep current of his thoughts; he spoke slowly, using cautious and reasonable terms. To reach our military goals, he added, we would need three times as many boots on the ground, which means: *three times as much funding*.

Step by step, he pulled his audience's consciousness onto more rational terrain than the preceding orators, as if his personal opinions didn't enter into it. As Pierre Cot had done that morning, but in more articulate, less polemical language, Mendès advanced unhurriedly, without ever giving his colleagues the sense that he was better than them. Solid and modest, his robust silhouette faced the Assembly. He turned his pages slowly, raising his head now and again. In those moments, his visage seemed to float on a murky background.

"The truth," Mendès resumed, with a closed and almost sad expression, "at a time when we are confronted with so many other challenges, is that we do not have the material resources to impose in Indochina the military solution that we have pursued for so long."

Suddenly, emotions became very heated. Even the most impenitent, the most hidebound, the most somnolent of parliamentarians, the ones who had looked dead for the past several sessions, understood that something was happening. And in fact, Mendès immediately proceeded to the famous budget deficit. He himself favored austerity measures, he always had, he amplified, with undeniable sincerity, looking surprised and genuine under his raised eyebrows. Politicians are adept at all manner of trickery; they always play the same part, and often badly. But sincerity makes an impression and leaves them disarmed. So that's it, they said to themselves: the war is too expensive.

It was then that the deputies, temporarily abandoning party instructions, setting aside intrigues and backroom haggling, briefly became *people* again, rather than *corporate brands*. Mendès's words entered into these men—oh, not miraculously or anything; but their rational impact and Mendès's frank, convincing tone could leave no bourgeois indifferent. Mendès knew how to talk to them, speak their language in the narrow confines of their interests. And that October 19, at 4 p.m., he tried to smuggle in something greater.

Still, despite an indisputable success—and you could feel it in the rows of benches, Mendès had scored, he had used the right words, he had shaken their prominent-citizen consciences—despite that, Mendès must suddenly have felt very alone. Of course, he completely doubted that he'd rally a majority to his cause that day, perhaps reassuring himself that it would pay off later; and armed with that conviction, he had written his speech.

But now, before the Assembly, another conviction guided him, a deeper, darker faith, that had come from the words themselves.

A face is always a deformity. Our ideas disfigure us. We resemble one another. And yet, from the heights of what we call with too much respect or compunction a forum, a word can for an instant split the normal concordance with oneself. And I imagine that, at that moment, our faces reflect us entirely, as if they have been painted on; and that the master's brush—wise, lucid, gifted with a mad ardor—can momentarily disrupt the narcissistic dialogue in which we all indulge, in the deepest recesses of our cave, in the pathetic lie that we repeat to ourselves, silent and alone, and by which we are forever misled. I imagine that by force of circumstance, of the drama that suddenly binds us to others violently and sadly, something gets disturbed in what we call our image; and that brutally, in the flash of an eclipse, we glimpse the persistent, denied, repressed dispute between this poor self-love that is buried but perpetually maintained by our ego and something else, something outside of us, something in everyone's interest: what was once called the truth of our times.

———

Thus, on that October 19, 1950, Mendès stepped out of line. His other face appeared. That serious, seemingly split face, the one we've been familiar with ever since. The face with its raised eyebrows, doubtful and exposed. It's so difficult to describe a face, a mix of flesh and thought. In Mendès's face, there is something reassuring and worried, fragile and Cartesian, tough and hesitant, which accounts for its charm. And when someone speaks the truth—in other words, gropes in the dark—you can feel it.

At that point, a shudder ran through the semicircular amphitheater, a kind of silent heave. The faces were surprised, tense. They had to avoid an incident at all costs. But they had no time to react, as Mendès had finally reached the key point of his speech: "The other solution," he said in his most nonconfrontational tones, "would be to reach a political accord—an accord, that is, with the people we're fighting."

Everyone immediately understood what he meant. The formula seemed logical, affable, even respectful, but for most of the deputies it comprised something inadmissible. Then Mendès raised his eyes again and looked at the throng of his colleagues. Some still seemed to be debating with themselves: "Negotiate with the Vietminh! That's a line in the sand we'll never cross," they thought. The government stirred on its bench. At that moment, Mendès felt the blood drain from his face. He became almost faint. Progressively, over the course of his speech, he had distanced himself from his party's positions, from the positions of the vast majority of the Assembly, even from the positions he himself had held until that moment; from the positions of his milieu, those of his social class, those of the grand coalition to which, without wanting to admit it, he belonged; from the positions that should one day have led him to occupy the place he deserved, and moreover that everyone predicted for him, the top spot, the presidency of the Council of Ministers. And he suddenly felt within himself a blank space, a breach between what he might be and what he was, between what he hoped to become and what he would become, between what he believed and what he had defended, between his loved ones and himself; and the certainty of what he'd just said now completely sank in, and he knew that he should absolutely not have said it, that it was in fact the very worst thing to say. And although he had said it skillfully and moderately, with the appropriate words, not mentioning any names that would rile people up; not mentioning colonialism, as Pierre Cot had that morning, or the Vietminh, or Ho Chi Minh; not even respectfully evoking *our* soldiers, *our* army, or the disaster at Cao Bang; in a tone ultimately so different from Daniel Mayer's, a tone that Old Herriot himself could have endorsed—nonetheless, he had said it. He had at that moment taken a new, radically isolated stance. And he knew immediately that he could not have said anything else.

He lifted his head. Looked over the amphitheater. At that moment, his large face was wide open. And it was as if the expression "the people's representative" sometimes actually meant something.

How Our Glorious Battles
Transform into Corporations

═══

Odd as it seems, there was not, and never had been, a French colony established in Cao Bang: no French quarter, no European social life, no enterprising shopkeeper, no adventurous hotelier, not a single advance man. Moreover, there weren't, and never had been, any Europeans in Dong Khe, or in Lang Son, or in Mao Khe, or in Lung Phai. The pewter mining company in Cao Bang had started in 1905. To function, it required only a few European engineers and foremen, and to keep itself protected it needed a military outpost. In 1911, it was apparently absorbed by Etains et Wolfram du Tonkin. That company, with a capital of three million eight hundred thousand francs, like any legal entity, had a head office, a legal domicile, very far from Upper Tonkin, very far from Cao Bang, but not very far from the National Assembly on Boulevard Haussmann in the eighth

arrondissement of Paris, and a mere few steps from the
Banque de l'Indochine, which owned a serious interest in
the business. Ten years later, its capital was seven million;
twelve years after that, twenty-four million; and on the
eve of the Second World War, an extraordinary thirty-six
million. So it was not for a simple outpost lost in some
jungle that the army was fighting, nor for a few French
colonials gone astray; and out of respect for exactitude,
we should rebaptize The Battle of Cao Bang, over which
the parliament was tearing itself apart, as: The Battle for
the Pewter Mining Company of Cao Bang, which would
confer on it its true importance.

But it's not only the Battle of Cao Bang that should
bear the name of a mining interest. The Battle of Mao
Khe, which took place a few months later, in March 1951,
could just as well be rebaptized The Battle for the French
Coal Mining Company of Tonkin. And in lieu of the
bloody combat we read about in books, they should also
relate, in a less romantic but ultimately more tragic vein,
how the four hundred troops, reinforced by the 6th Battalion of Colonial Paratroopers, three destroyers, two
landing craft, and ultimately bombers and fighter planes,
responded to the harrowing call made to it from Paris, at
a scale we cannot see; and also tell of the twenty thousand
hectares over which extended the coalfields of Mao Khe,
which at the time were divided up into 78,760 shares.

And, were we to mix Homer with market economics, we could sing of the 393 million in capital that were valiantly defended by the B-26 bombers and Hellcat fighter planes, since it was indeed, and no mistaking, at the coal mines that the Vietminh had launched their attack.

As for the Battle of Ninh Binh three months later, let us celebrate without undue bombast the intrepid Battle for the Coal Mining Company of Ninh Binh. And wasn't the one in Hoa Binh in December 1951 also about capital and revenues? Couldn't we rebaptize it The Battle for the Gold Mine Company of Hoa Binh? We'd understand much better the fury of the skirmishes. And wasn't the famous Battle of Dong Trieu waged by both the French Expeditionary Corps and the Chamber of the Commerce of the Seine? And the fifty-one dead of the 6th Battalion of Colonial Paratroopers: were they sacrificed for France, or for Mr. Pierre-Charles Bastid, board member of the coal mining company Société Anonyme des Charbonnages, CEO of Etains et Wolfram du Tonkin, CEO of Etains de Pia-Ouac, engineering consultant to the Banque de l'Indochine, director of Etablissements Eiffel and of Mines d'Or d'Outre-Mer, the overseas gold-mine authority—weren't they really fighting for him? And were the true generals in that battle named Jean de Lattre de Tassigny and Raoul Salan, or in fact Varenne, Etienne, Bastid, and Moreau-Defarges, board members of the coal-mining concern; and shouldn't we in fact call it *The Battle for the Coal Mining Company of Dong Trieu*, whose bank account (no. 38056) was located, as were no doubt all the others, at the Banque de l'Indochine, 96 Boulevard Haussmann, Paris? And that is how our heroic battles are transformed one by one into faceless corporations.

The Nabob of Eure-et-Loir

T he session lasted until 7 p.m.; then it adjourned, resumed at 9 p.m., and absolutely nothing happened
until 10 p.m. Naturally, the Communists and all the
other deputies hurled copious insults at each other, but
really nothing of note happened; it was the start of a
normal evening. When the painful feelings had subsided
and Mendès's arguments had evaporated beneath the
large glass roof, the deputies contented themselves with
a round-trip from bench to bar; and once you'd sipped
your martini, a pal towed you back to the amphitheater,
where you kept up the conversation in whispers.

Suddenly, at around 10:10, Maurice Viollette opened
his mouth. He was slated for the open discussion, and
now it was his turn. He was surely the main political
figure from the Eure-et-Loir region in the twentieth
century, which means both a lot and little. The man
who stood up that October 19 superlatively incarnated
the Eure-et-Loir, an amalgam of industry, wheat, and

livestock. As mayor of Dreux, he reigned over his region for fifty years, the big boss of the tobacconists, the caid of Orgères-en-Beauce, the Charlemagne of Châteaudun. When he stood up—his body at once heavy and dry, like most old people's—Maurice Viollette was eighty years old. He had been a deputy since 1902. He was minister of provisions during the First World War and governor general of Algeria under the Leftist Cartel. It was therefore an authority, no, a monument, that gathered itself up and rose at ten minutes past ten that evening, October 19, 1950. But we must still put a face to that summary description, place a head on the suit. Maurice Viollette did not have a mug to match his name; the disparity between name and face was total. As much as the name Viollette was engaging, gentle, even amusing, so his face was repellent, harsh, verging on evil.

Maurice Viollette stood up: his only way of imposing silence. At that moment, he represented what we might call, in bombastified vocabulary, a *moral authority*. His speech was intended for Pierre Mendès France; its aim was to nullify the effect Mendès had produced, wipe away the affront. "The day when our combatants in Indochina learn that we have reached a settlement with their enemies," the patriarch stated in a tone dripping with gravitas, "the day they learn that we are thinking of negotiating a kind of armistice such as the one in 1940, the weapons will fall from their hands." Then he added, stressing his conceit: "No! I beg of you." The center and the right clapped loudly, and there was even a smattering of applause from the left-wing benches.

There is a moment in politics when convictions fail and good intentions run aground. At that point, no matter if one has been a *progressive* colonial administrator, as Maurice Viollette had been for a time; no matter if one has been a defender of human rights, concerned with the fate of indigenous populations; no matter if one bequeaths three hundred thousand francs to one's home town, the spin-off from which is to be distributed each year to the needy families of the canton; no matter if one has donated one's bourgeois residence to the good town of Dreux; no matter if one has drafted these codicils in one's winter garden, between a clove tree and a moribund avocado; no matter if one has gifted such and such a charitable organization one's Barbedienne pendulum clock, in cherry marble and bronze; and no matter if it decorated your bedroom in Janville, your baronial mansion in Dreux, or the waiting room of your office in Chartres: the main thing resides in the perfect alignment of it all; the main thing stands on either side of the sconces in your living room, between the lions' heads with rings in their chompers.

Our dishware, the quality of our table settings, our napkin rings and ice cube trays, say as much about us as our opinions. We are the items we possess. And the very fact of possessing takes us very far. To the point where we have to listen to the words of Maurice Viollette a second time in order to gauge their violence: "The day when our combatants in Indochina learn that we have reached a settlement with their enemies, the day they learn that we are thinking of negotiating a kind of armistice such as the one in 1940, the weapons will fall from their hands."

The important thing here is not the dismay of the soldiers, most of whom (as Chérif Djemad had earlier pointed out) came from North Africa, but the battalions of colonials; and it was surely not love of country that sent them to Indochina. The important part comes down to an analogy. Maurice Viollette compares. He gauges Pierre Mendès France's attitude toward the past and evaluates Mendès's proposal by juxtaposing it with another event: June 1940.

And thus, surreptitiously, he likens Pierre Mendès France to those who made peace with the Germans, to Laval and Pétain. How strange! How bizarre that comparison is, and how offensive! Those applauding on left and right don't seem to notice. Frédéric-Dupont, red-faced from his drinks at the bar, jubilates. He no doubt finds it perfectly reasonable to assimilate Mendès's views with the defeatism of June 1940, as will Edmond Michelet when he reprises the anathema two hours later. Michelet, moreover, will take advantage of his tirade to lash out at the Socialists and call them to order as well. After all, if Mendès had remained isolated, playing the lone moral sentinel, it wouldn't really matter. But he threatened to tip the Socialist camp to his side, which would have toppled the grand coalition.

Edmond Michelet: "The attitude of Mr. Mendès France, which, I repeat, has been approved by the Socialists, is one of abandonment, in other words, of Vichy."

Protests on the left and center.

The president: "Order!"

Edmond Michelet: "We have to call a spade a spade." (Renewed protests.) "I say that any current policy of capitulation in Indochina would be just like Vichy."

Night has fallen. Mendès listens impassively. He takes it in. But inside the man, behind his genuine modesty, his countenance, a spark must have floated in the ashes. Perhaps it was then that he remembered the catalogue of the antisemitic exhibit organized in 1941 by the magazine *L'Illustration* at the Palais Berlitz: he was in hiding, living under an assumed name, disguised in a ratty suit and a beret, makeup, and a mustache, and in amazement he recognized himself among the exhibited mannequins, incarnating *The Jew*. Of course, capitulation always refers to *Munich* or *Vichy*, the commonplaces of courtroom rhetoric; but in this case, addressed to Mendès, whose life had been under threat, and as a political figure, and as a Jew, the accusation is patently reprehensible. When Edmond Michelet evokes Vichy while pointing at Mendès, smack in the middle of the Assembly, secure in his authority and his effect, insidiously assimilating the man's political position with that of the Pétain regime, he is drawing a parallel that is inappropriate and obscene. He is likening Mendès to those who sought to kill him.

———

FRENCH TEXTBOOKS define the Fourth Republic by its instability, rehashing the Gaullist thesis and never testing it against the facts. In reality, and despite the governmental musical chairs, a closer look reveals a furious continuity. The governments of the Fourth Republic exist in a vacuum, as if one were constantly shuffling the same slips of paper in the same drum. As such, Bidault was minister of foreign affairs under Ramadier administrations I and II and Schuman administration I; then he was President of the Council of Ministers and Vice-President of the Governmental Council under Queuille

II and III, Pleven II, and Edgar Faure I; again Minister of Foreign Affairs under Mayer I and finally under Laniel I—such that in spite of the apparent discontinuities, over a period of seven years, he was in the government for nearly five of them. And we could say the same for all of them, for Teitgen, Faure, Pleven, Mayer; we could follow their major or minor appointments within the governmental edifice, as if their differences, the oppositions they energetically staged each and every day, were but modest variations of the same concept: that the Republic was no more than a limited combination of opinions by which they were handed the leading roles, united and immutable, eternity in the heart of time.

As for the nomenclature of these administrations, they sound like a pharaonic succession: Schuman I, Schuman II, Queuille I, Bidault II, Bidault III, Queuille II. And under Queuille I, Edgar Faure was Minister of Finance, Jules Moch of the Interior, Schuman of Foreign Affairs, Ramadier of National Defense; then under Bidault II, Queuille was Vice-President of the Council, Schuman remained in Foreign Affairs, Jules Moch in Interior, Edgar Faure in Finance, and René Mayer became Keeper of the Seals. And we could go on like this for hours, during which the same ten or fifteen members of the club of Council presidents would parade by like zodiac signs in the firmament.

And if we pay close attention to this great stability, this immense edifice that is power, this vast community of clichés, interests, and careers, the dissonant tirades of Maurice Viollette and Edmond Michelet suddenly take on larger significance, become more than just tactless asides or isolated rhetorical flourishes, tone-deaf or repulsive as they may be. For Viollette is a radical, like Mendès; he too had been a minister under the Popular Front, and so the virulence of his attack seems surprising. Moreover, it was picked up again two hours later by Michelet, who was in the Resistance like Mendès, who saved Jewish lives during the war by providing forged papers, who was even sent to Dachau. If we look only at the protagonists, close up, we can't understand. In order to grasp what's going on, we have to widen our field of vision, ponder the entire edifice, examine the thick, massive, allegorical object that is the Palais Bourbon, seat of the National Assembly.

The stones are cold. The figure of the Republic stands quietly in its marble niche. Pigeons snooze beneath the friezes. Red velvet ropes, defending the patrimony, keep you from getting too close to the statuary. Everything is cleaned and polished. The ancient legislators stand in the four corners of the room, behind the backs of the guards. Every morning, a brigade of cleaning staff dust off Jaurès's collar, wipe Albert de Mun's lips, shine their marble shoes. And so, on that October 19, 1950, it was perhaps not strictly Viollette who was trying to intimidate Mendès, perhaps not Michelet who uttered those offensive words, but the very stability of the edifice that took them as spokespersons; it was the political regime itself that addressed Mendès through their mouths, that made them solemnly lift their voices and pronounce those strange and threatening sentences.

Maurice Viollette is old, terribly old; he seems exhausted under the pale light of the huge glass canopy. Facing that multitude of approving faces, he is like a feather in the wind, a straw on the waves, and he lets himself be carried away by their approbation. Deputies have risen to their feet to applaud him. It isn't like for Juge that morning, or for Chérif Djemad, whom nobody listened to; at this moment, everyone is riveted, Frédéric-Dupont is jubilant, Max Brusset is jubilant, the entire semicircular amphitheater is hanging on his words. And so Maurice Viollette frees himself from the past, forgets Léon Blum's face, forgets the man's gentleness and determination: all of it fades under the encouragements of his colleagues. He forgets the insults he had to endure, the cries of hatred: "Death to Blum! String him up!" He forgets the thugs who, on February 13, 1936, pounced on the future

Council president as he left the Assembly, attacking his car, ripping off its headlight, smashing in the rear window and wounding Léon Blum in the head, which was soon covered in blood. He forgets the paid vacations and salary increases he had once defended, the pension plan for miners, his support for the Spanish Republicans. He even forgets the curious prewar insult hurled against him at the time: *anti-French*. And in a kind of strange intoxication, brushing aside the pain he'd just felt, banishing from his memory Blum's face, the sad, intelligent smile that briefly came to mind as he took the final step, like the indulgent and fraternal sign of the best of himself; forgetting the children he never had, the tenderness he'd never known, the people he had loved, he felt an unpleasant rigidity overtake his entire being, and he pursued his harangue all the more vehemently:

"No doubt, people say: war!" the old man shouted in an unexpected resumption. "Only, beware: in trying to avoid one war, you will start many," he roared. "If you make the error of initiating negotiations, of abdicating to Ho Chi Minh, tomorrow you will have to abdicate in Madagascar, in Tunisia, in Algeria. And perhaps," he growled to a mesmerized audience, "there might be those who say that, all things considered, the frontier of the Vosges is all France needs. When you go from abdication to abdication, you are heading for catastrophe and even for dishonor." Numerous benches display their approval with hearty applause. Tongues wag furiously, people are inordinately animated, good manners melt away like a cake of soap. And Viollette finally ends his speech with an appalling, almost fantastic warning: "Any weakness on our part will lead to the collapse of our nation."

This time, the applause is lively and sustained, right, left, and center. The play is a success, it should have a good run. And indeed, it will stay on the bill for four more years.

Meet the Press

Every day, we read a page in the book of our lives, but it's not the right one. And every day, we start again. Thus, after the disaster at Cao Bang, as if a top-ranking military man could change the course of events, they appointed Jean de Lattre de Tassigny high commissioner and commander in chief in Indochina. He arrived in Saigon in early December, rapidly developed the Vietnamese National Army, and with it won ephemeral victories by means of unprecedented concentrations of troops and bombardments with napalm, which he was among the first to use on a grand scale.

Finally, de Lattre circled the globe to defend the cause of Indochina, aka the free world. He met with Truman in Washington, the pope in Rome. But the undeniable apogee of his tour was neither his thirty minutes at the White House nor his visit to the Vatican but, rather, his improbable appearance on NBC's widely viewed political program *Meet the Press*.

It was with tact, amiability, and flawless French that Henry Cabot Lodge ushered de Lattre backstage. The general admitted his nervousness—his English was so poor, and besides, he'd never been on TV before! Lodge reassured him: the interviewers would be friendly, the show's reputation for putting its subjects through the wringer was overrated. Certain questions might seem direct, strictly for the audience's benefit, but hadn't they promised not to overstep the bounds of his previous interviews? That's true. De Lattre sighed with relief. They introduced him to the makeup crew; he shook their hands automatically, then settled into the huge faux-leather armchair. An assistant turned the control knob and the chair rose and rose. De Lattre leaned back and closed his eyes. There was no one around. Not a sound. Even Cabot Lodge was gone. De Lattre relaxed his arms on the wide rests, head thrown back. General! For an instant, he felt as if he was encased in straw, it was so hot! Good God, what sun! He opened one eye, found himself facing a brace of neons; the makeup artist was studying him as she ringed his neck with tissues.

Suddenly, the star anchor of *Meet the Press*, Martha Rountree, enters the makeup room. She murmurs words of welcome that de Lattre doesn't understand. They translate for him—it was actually in French, she had taken the trouble to learn a polite phrase. The general stands up too quickly and nearly falls off his large chair; once on his feet, he repeats at every opportunity: "I am very pleased to be here," nodding his head mechanically. Next to the American anchor's ease, his stiffness is painful to see. Finally, after several muted pleasantries, Miss Rountree leads de Lattre to the dais and invites him to take a seat beside her. Roll the opening credits.

Under the spotlights, facing the audience, de Lattre suddenly feels himself wilt; his stomach hurts, his trousers are too tight, he nervously straightens his tie. Lodge has told him that the broadcast could reach more than ten million viewers and that it would probably be shown, at the Pentagon's impetus, on about forty channels. Right now, he finds that good news terrifying—forty channels!

Miss Rountree: "Good afternoon, ladies and gentlemen, members of the press panel, and our very special guest, General de Lattre. It's a good thing we have Senator Lodge here today because my French isn't very good." After this friendly little preamble, Martha Rountree, the merciless Martha Rountree, in clear, silver-tongued tones that perfectly embody the success, rationality, and fake transparency of journalism, pivots without undue transition: "Now I think we'll let Mr. Spivak have the first question."

Spivak: "General, I know this trip of yours to the US is not a pleasure trip. Are you seeking aid from us for your war in Indochina?"

The question is indeed direct. The saliva suddenly drains from the general's mouth. And yet, despite his lips sticking to his teeth, despite his constricted throat and the anxiety squeezing his gut, de Lattre begins to speak: "*I shall answer in one minute. But before, will you allow me to say something? My English is poor, very poor.*" The written transcript of his words does not convey the dizziness he's feeling. You have to see and hear him. In a staccato voice, de Lattre stammers and fidgets: "*You know, I came here in the spirit of a Chief, military chief, was as I told you, the responsibility of the great battle…*"— and there, ellipsis, de Lattre sinks into the quicksand of words, and no one understands a thing he says. For all his arm-waving and pugnacious bravado, his words are meaningless, and he continues in freefall for a moment, completely lost in this foreign tongue, a thousand leagues from any clear signification, splashing about in the primordial ocean of signs.

———

Finally, de Lattre gets hold of himself, and his phrases come back to him, especially the crucial thing he absolutely must say, even amid the pure gibberish; the sentence his advisers made him rehearse over and over, and that Cabot Lodge taught him how to pronounce with as un-disastrous an accent as possible, so that he wouldn't forget to say it on the set. And now it returns to his mind, and even if it's not the right moment, better to put it out there than to forget it altogether. And so, fists forward, hammering out his words, de Lattre declares: "*I did not come to ask American soldiers.*"

The American audience must have been flabbergasted. Was this some kind of joke? Even Volapük is spoken by some twenty people worldwide, but de Lattre's English has only a single interlocutor, the general himself. Here he is, speaking live to ten million Americans, in prodigious double-talk, vertiginous nonsense. It's as if History in person were speaking, with its pendulum-shaped glottis and its lacerating teeth. And yet, the audience, aided by countless commentaries, will retain the essential point: that de Lattre came here to ask not for American soldiers but simply for arms and equipment. It's enough to make this General Tapioca with his caustic voice rather likable: he hasn't come to take away our children!

The interview drags on, the hands of the clock advance, and Spivak leans forward energetically, as if about to ask *the* question that we've all been waiting for. Spivak is good, really good; he knows how to make it look like he's going to be blunt, without kid gloves, and the disengagement his eyes seem to convey is like a guarantee of impartiality: "Can you tell us now what the importance of Indochina is to us, to Americans?"

As usual, the question sounds trenchant, but actually it's a softball. As if it had been written by the army's own Communications office. And yet, de Lattre gets bogged down, can't find the words. At that moment, any words would do, any old forgotten word, even a jerk or a sigh. De Lattre gropes his way across the desert of language, between the sand of words and the wind of meaning. He has fallen into a kind of silent storm. Not a sound. Where are all those little words that Cabot Lodge painstakingly taught him and made him repeat one last time, in the bathroom, mere moments ago? Desperately seeking them on his scalp, he runs a hand through his hair, but the gel is too heavy and his hair sticks. Then, as if bursting out of the water, the general catches his breath and adds "that Indochina and especially…was the keystone of Southeast Asia, and that keystone was framed…"

————

Oof! The statement is almost clear. The journalists are relieved. But barely have they inwardly congratulated themselves on returning to the standards of mainstream TV than the general flounders again. Why the hell is he still talking, that was quite enough! Spivak would gladly lend him a hand, but he can't pull off his magic trick alone, it would be too obvious, too much like hot-dogging. He needs a partner, and that's when Cabot Lodge comes in. His role is practical, neutral; he seems to be there just to lend a hand, as if his only interest in the matter were to help out an old friend and act as interpreter before the cameras.

And so, as if he wants to elicit a necessary extra detail, as if speaking for all those who do not yet have enough background information and want, as honestly as pie, to know more, Cabot Lodge asks his old buddy: "You mean if Indochina falls, all of Southeast Asia is lost."

De Lattre: "Yes I think so. If you want, I can explain why."

No thanks! The stagehands quietly dance their ballet, skipping over the mass of cables, creeping up on tiptoe. And without missing a beat, Spivak gets things back on track; straightening his handsome striped tie, he in turn tosses de Lattre a life preserver: "Do you think that is important to us, for example, as Korea?"

And here, the general might be clumsy, mind-bogglingly clumsy, but even he can't help grasping the helping hand. Besides, hadn't he already rehearsed this little duet with Lodge?

De Lattre: "I think that there is not only parallel to make between Korea and Indochina," he abruptly emits, with a learned air. "It is exactly the same." At that moment, de Lattre has got his routine down pat, he'll be able to say a few words that are simple but pregnant with meaning. He makes bizarre, sweeping gestures, with stiff lyrical eloquence: "In Korea," he adds, confident in the effect he's producing, "you are fighting against Communists. In Indochina we are fighting against Communists." Sometimes the simplest comparisons are the most striking. "Korea War, Indochina War, it is the same war." Q.E.D.

———

GOOD LORD, a television program is long, and it's so hot in the NBC studios, and those stagehands with their constant back and forth, can't they sit still! De Lattre is tense, horribly tense. The lights are stifling. The spotlights move around like wandering stars.

Finally, McDaniel takes the questioning baton. He addresses the general softly, but his question stings a little more than expected: "General de Lattre, at least one or two years ago the war in Indochina we understood was not popular in your own country…"

General de Lattre: "I shall answer you very clearly. You see, we are making in Indochina at the moment a war which is absolutely without material interest for my country. We have given to the associated nations their independence, and I tell you with all my loyalty, that the independence is not a word, it is a real fact."

There it is, de Lattre managed to get out the crucial word: *independence.* And without even having to utter the phrase *colonial war.* It's too good an opportunity to waste: Senator Lodge grabs it on the fly, and in his clearest, gentlest tones, he reformulates, seemingly as a question, the key point of the statement, the message that the audience absolutely must retain. In a firm but lofty voice, that of the Cabot clan, operating a very delicate shift in timbre, he articulates: "The states of Indochina now have their independence, is that what you mean?"

The Cabots were made for this. Ever since their ancestors definitively posed their rumps in a comfortable armchair after earning enough boodle so as not to have to lift an effing finger for a good hundred generations; ever since they became part of high society, they've been yakking. And you have to have heard Henry Cabot Lodge address the United Nations to know how prepotent, how characteristic his language is; to really see how the French tongue, not to mention the Spanish, Russian, or even Chinese, is but a folk idiom in comparison, dialects reduced to the rank of local or provincial phenomena by the superiorly warm and icy voices of the Cabots.

It was then that, as a consummate professional, Martha Rountree changed her tone for a note of pathos, brief but effective, and suddenly threw at the general: "I understand your own son was killed, General."

"Yes," answered de Lattre.

"That was very recently, wasn't it?"

"On the night of the 30th of May."

Rain flows down the window panes. The rain of Saigon. The rain. At this moment, the general is alone in a small boat rotting along the shore. The studio is filled with mist, fog coats the spotlights. De Lattre stares at an invisible point. But the show goes on. You display someone's private life, then wrap it up like a slice of cheese. And questions follow on questions, and de Lattre answers, loses his way, answers, gets mired in the English language as if in a tropical rainforest. Finally, apropos the development of a Vietnamese army, Lodge nudges him gently out of his retrenchment, asking him to overplay the score of the troop leader, seeking to highlight his manly tone, without which things were about to get boring: "You mean they are good soldiers and you can make paratroopers out of these native soldiers?"

"Paratroops?" exclaims de Lattre. "I think there is no youth in the world so ready to make so quick paratroopers." But once he's awkwardly emitted this flat compliment, he can't help making a bad joke about the size of the Indochinese, who because of their light weight take too long to reach the ground. At that moment, the door swings open and we can see the everyday racism of the army, reminiscent of the brief note written three years earlier, after a report by his old comrade General Valluy, in which de Lattre said: "There's the problem of the Indochinese—(Laotian) (Cambodian)…weak, very different from those little Annamite monkeys."

After a further series of questions, the program comes to a close. Miss Rountree interrupts the general at the prescribed moment, the conclusive moment, in mid-sentence. She very politely thanks de Lattre and Senator Lodge and ends by complimenting the general on his English.

An Honorable Exit

The war, with its litany of violence, stretched from the earliest days of France's conquest, so intensely do people dislike being subjugated. But after 1945, as French power declined, it became increasingly difficult to maintain its presence there; and after the disaster at Cao Bang, the colony's fate appeared to be sealed. The war was indeed too expensive. Public opinion grew weary of it. De Lattre's meager victories had required an inordinate mobilization for paltry results. And then de Lattre died, and so they had to find something else. The expression you heard most often, the typical retort, the refrain that seemed to be on everyone's lips, was the hope for *an honorable exit*. But it was rather awkward. We had become mired so deeply in the language of duties and responsibilities over the past eight years. Once more, then, they adopted a solemn attitude, since this difficult task—relaunch the war to finally end it, recapture Indochina before leaving it—required that they find *someone*. Seven commanders in chief had already succeeded one another. There had been the great Leclerc, Valluy, Salan ad interim, Blaizot, Carpentier, de Lattre, and again Salan ad interim. They appointed an eighth, General Henri Navarre. They appointed him to find an unfindable solution, to a position that no one wanted.

Henri Navarre was learned, caustic, self-assured, and cold, or so they say. His mother was related on one side to Murat; the other side had grown rich refining sugar in the Calvados region. This bourgeois dynasty had been, by turns, moderate republicans during the Republic, then conservative under the Second Empire, and when that fell they'd supported the republican and colonialist Ferry. It was said that they owned some forty buildings in Paris and had gotten mixed up in various stock market manipulations. It was also said that one of Navarre's ancestors, having become a widow, moved alone into a small two-room apartment near the Gare Saint-Lazare and with her own money funded lodgings for working families; good for her.

When Navarre was reaching maturity, he attended preparatory classes for the Saint-Cyr Military Academy, in cavalry. He had learned to ride a horse on his grandfather's property, between alleys of plane trees and rows of box trees. He was awarded the Croix de Guerre in 1918, served in Syria and Germany, and supposedly helped plan, in 1939, a suicide assassination plot against Adolf Hitler. Then he followed Weygand to Algiers before going underground in 1942. After the war, he found himself in Germany, then in Algeria, then again in Germany, and it was in May 1953 that he was named commander in chief of the French forces in Indochina. He therefore packed his bags and left France. He was just shy of fifty-five. And this is where we find him, intelligent, with a talent for explaining things clearly, and maybe a bit stuck-up; the ministers saw him as a refined soldier who could behave himself in society. Henri Navarre was short—not terribly short, but short. I get this from a photo in which he's sticking a medal on Cogny's chest. He's a good head shorter and has the bearing of a little girl, with a curiously pinched expression on his face.

But who was Navarre? I don't know, no one knows, however many documents, letters, notes, books, and photos we might have. Even if we'd lived in the same cell with him for thirty years; even if we'd been his father, son, or wife; even if we'd been Navarre himself, we still might not know, or at least not know enough. An entire book wouldn't suffice to explain all the lineaments, hesitations, dejections, frustrations, and bizarre obstinacies in a single day of Henri Navarre's life. Not that his profound being was so hidden or complicated or shrouded in mystery, but there's something that glides over this man like sand in our sheets. A commander in chief is a blend of misplaced honor, small grievances, great pride—like the rest of us, basically—but all of it stuffed into a uniform, kneaded and molded, concealed, fucked up with outmoded values that we now have a hard time understanding or even identifying. In 1953, they were still just barely emerging from the Ancien Régime. Yes, in the armed forces, they were still thinking about cavalry spurs. I'll give an example. In '44, Navarre moved fast. On his orders, Captain de Castries's tanks took Karlsruhe twenty-four hours before the arrival of de Lattre, who never forgave him for it. Poor booboo.

A Visit to Matignon

―――――――

And so they drove the general to the mansion of the president of the Council of Ministers. Thunder rumbled in the distance. Place de la Concorde looked puny. The Obelisk was ugly. Crossing the Seine between two sheets of rain, Navarre rehashed over and over in his mind a slew of things he might possibly say. His small feet were hurting in the new shoes he'd put on that morning, which he now regretted. He posed his manicured hand on the leather elbow rest. A red light stopped the car just in front of the Assembly, but the raindrops on the window masked the façade; he stupidly tried to wipe them away.

Having passed through the monumental entryway of the Hotel Matignon, they parked in the courtyard. General Navarre emerged smartly from the vehicle, thrusting both legs from the car in a single motion, then swinging his small body outside.

The Council president, René Mayer, greeted the general. He was broad-shouldered, tall, affable, a businessman dabbling in politics. At first Navarre found himself gratified with a whole symphony of blandishments, and he listened gravely. They took a short stroll around the garden. Mayer dragged the general toward the alley of lindens. "The situation in Indochina is quite simply a disaster," he confessed. "The war is all but lost. The best we can hope for is *an honorable exit.*"

Once they'd left the alley of lindens, the Council president raised his head, and in a brusque but cordial tone declared to the general that *he could absolutely count on him*; then, modestly, as if coming up for air, with that hometown demeanor he often assumed, he glanced at Navarre, holding his unlit pipe in one hand, in a kind of instinctive arbitration between a touch of familiarity that was not devoid of charm and the dignity of his office: "Although I'm perfectly aware of the difficulty of the mission I'm sending you on," he murmured, "I must nonetheless caution you against any untimely requests for reinforcements"—those last words spoken as if the bad news added a certain distinction to the confidence he placed in the man.

Their feet trod the wide lawn. The Council president said some more about the "demanding task" facing Navarre; then, turning slowly to face him, he added that his great military experience was "indispensable" to them. Navarre believed it. He felt a dead weight lift inside him, and saw himself enlarged in his own esteem. Finally, Mayer clearly enunciated Navarre's appointment. The latter voiced a few reservations: "I don't know the terrain."

"So much the better," Mayer shot back. "You'll see it more clearly."

The Navarre Plan

S everal hours later, in the back of the car bringing him to the airport, Navarre was almost amazed that Providence had taken so long to offer him this post. But when he landed in Indochina, he learned that Salan's departure had precipitated a huge exodus. The members of de Lattre's team were all returning to France; it was every man for himself. They let him know that his appointment didn't inspire much confidence, that only de Lattre could have carried out the perilous mission he'd been assigned. He felt a shiver of jealousy. He let nothing show but adopted an even firmer tone.

Persecuted by the blasts from the air conditioner, Navarre passes his hand repeatedly over his flat gray hair. His face is transparent and flaccid. He's too hot, but the conditioned air is making his throat sore. His small hazel eyes come to rest on everyone without holding anyone's gaze. Among the top brass, General Cogny, commanding the north zone of the delta, has been warmly recommended to him by members of the government. Not knowing what else to do, Navarre decides to lean on the only superior officer who isn't abandoning ship. When he tells Cogny of his promotion to the rank of major general, the colossus in Bermuda shorts cries out in a burst of emotion, "You won't regret this!" But Navarre cares little for the gratitude of subordinates.

After several weeks spent inspecting the units and looking over the charts, the commander in chief feels he knows the terrain well enough. Indochina is now just a background on a map; he has located and noted its rivers, mountains, and vast forests. Indochina is sitting there, alone before him, on a grid. He gazes at it; the graphic conventions slowly become realities for him, and no doubt he slips from a world of study into his fantasy. At this point, Indochina is the epicenter of something: an anxiety; an aphasic, silent, greedy desire.

The first act of his plan would unfold during the campaign of 1953–1954, which had barely begun: it was about avoiding confrontations, developing a local army to support our troops, and reconstituting a large, mobile field force. The second act would occur the following year: using this field force, which they'd have had time to train, they'd try to inflict such a defeat on the enemy that France would be in an advantageous position to negotiate—the famous *honorable exit*. Concerning the future strategy of the Vietminh, the general put forward three hypotheses in the margins of his plan: a surge on the Red River Delta, a push toward the south, or a push toward Upper Laos. This latter hypothesis was the most painful. It was with regard to it that they first mentioned the name Dien Bien Phu.

In July, on his return to France, General Navarre outlined his plan to the Committee of the Chiefs of Staff, then to the National Defense Committee. They smoked a few good cigars, a spot of brandy warmed everyone's cockles. Several bald heads formed a corolla around a large-scale map. Navarre summarized. He said a few words in memory of his father, an old professor of Greek, spoke smilingly about the Peloponnese; finally, from the Calydonian Boar, he slid imperceptibly to the Vietminh. The beast's bristles, stiff as rigid spears, were transformed sentence by sentence into a concrete menace; the hoarse grunts of Ovid's telling, as Navarre exposed his plan, evoked the increasingly numerous attacks in the Delta; its breath that scorched the boughs personified the new weapons the Vietminh might have. Everyone pulled inward. Throats were cleared. The demonstration was elegant.

After a long, muddled discussion of the questions raised by this detailed exposition, the committee members agreed in concert that although the plan really seemed like a little jewel, a masterpiece of prudence and military strategy, it was nonetheless "too costly." One does have to watch one's pennies, you know, and you can't go around bombing everything in sight without having to pay the bill sooner or later, send a little check to the arms dealer. They showered him with compliments, but he was nonetheless asked to revise his plan *downward*. They evoked the aid from America, already pretty steep, and even more generous since General de Lattre's goodwill tour, as the United States was now underwriting a good 40 percent of the war's cost; needless to say, they were soon going to ask for more. But in the meantime, they needed a more economical plan, a discount plan.

Couldn't he try a little harder, painful as it was—but after all, budget constraints are budget constraints—couldn't he envision something a bit more modest, and cheaper? They asked General Navarre to give it a think. Mortified, he returned to Saigon in early August to formulate a new proposal. It repelled him to have to pare down the wings of his great chimera. And so he opted to think about something else, distract himself; and the ceremonies followed in frenetic succession during the first part of his reign. The commander in chief started by pinning decorations on every available torso. A supplemental palm on the Croix de Guerre for Cogny, Gilles, Ducournau, and Rabertin. God, how he loved hoisting himself up on tiptoe to their powerful chests! Navarre looked like a little boy, applying himself to the task.

At the end of October, Navarre received some strange news. The Vietminh high command seemed to have given up on attacking the delta and instead was deploying the 316th Division toward Laos. This was it, the fantasy was becoming flesh, the tables were turning, the tall grass was growing beneath his feet! Nothing Navarre could do, reality was dragging him along, everything seemed to be listing toward the worst outcomes. France had just committed itself to defend Laos; and Navarre imagined that the government's silence must be deciphered. Then he thought he heard a voice, a thin trickle of gold from which curious words flowed. And what did that voice say? It intoned: "Go to the heart of the great forest. Stop the Vietminh from occupying the rice fields of Dien Bien Phu. Don't forget that it's the only valley in that whole jungle, that it's the crossroads of East and West!" Navarre couldn't believe his reptilian brain and was overcome by vertigo. Yes, it was a revelation: they must cover Northern Laos. Fearing another attack in the delta, General Cogny did not want him to redeploy all his troops and at first pleaded for a small operation, a mini–Dien Bien Phu. But Navarre was envisioning some huge carnivorous beast, extinct races, flowers harvested in springtime, harsh summers, sad autumns. He longed to experience an endless train of sorrows and glories. And suddenly, everything tipped overboard, and Navarre passed quickly from Dien Bien Phu 1.0, intended simply to block the Vietminh from getting to Laos, to something much more robust. What they needed was an entrenched camp. Not some piddly little thing where you got bored silly. No, a whole citadel of canvas and barbed wire. Cogny demurred, talked of a sinkhole of battalions. But at this point, Navarre didn't give a shit about Cogny; it's even as if the one's resistance reinforced the other's will. He feared he might blow a chance at victory. And this is how men stray into catastrophe.

The Installation

The valley of Dien Bien Phu had seen quite a few armies march through it: French troops, maybe Japanese troops, certainly Chinese troops, Siamese mahouts, Marco Polo's caravan. But for some time now, the valley had been peaceful. People grew rice there, and spinach, and papaya. Cattle grazed near the river, meek and faithful companions. And now all of a sudden, because some French general had decided to rendezvous here with the specter of warfare, they were going to make a sweep of the whole valley, riddle it with bunkers, raze dozens of villages, chase thousands of inhabitants into the hills, cut down trees, and burn the crops. They were going to obliterate any number of souvenirs, practices, hidden paths where lovers met in secret, fragile stone walls where children concealed tiny treasures.

On Friday, November 20, 1953, clumps of flowers, little blue canvas circles, lightweight jellyfish fell from the sky and flitted above the lush valley. The peasants watched these carnation petals drop, some eighteen hundred of them—with two batteries of air-lifted artillery and two heavy mortar companies. The next day, a bulldozer dropped from the sky. Immediately they went to work. The first task was to level out the old landing strip the Vietminh had demolished. A military film shows some soldiers, shirtless, having fun driving a small backhoe through the fields. And yet, the battle had already begun the day before: eleven French dead, one hundred Vietminh.

At the end of January, everything was ready. The command post was sunk belowground. They'd dug shelters, traced out trenches, and unspooled huge rolls of barbed wire to surround it all. Ten thousand men already lived here. And every day, they delivered tanks, jeeps, trucks, advance surgical units, copies of *Playboy*, and dumpster loads of canned food.

Christian Marie Ferdinand
de La Croix de Castries

They talk of a garden party seducer, of a locker stuffed with crumpled handkerchiefs and gambling debts. Yes, they say he fucked around quite a bit, Marie Ferdinand de La Croix de Castries, that his skinny little body contorted into dreadful positions, but always the same ones, on tiptoe. Of course, he didn't need a stepladder, Marie Ferdinand de La Croix de Castries, he managed just fine when mounting his American ladies. He wore a red scarf around his neck, and while the women bawled out their words of love, he kept a firm hold on his riding crop. But once Marie Ferdinand de La Croix de Castries had ejected his little sac of sperm, he gently laid down his crop next to his Malaysian sabre. Oh, he was an odd duck, that Marie Ferdinand de La Croix de Castries. They say he listened unmoved to the most tragic tales but looked downright grave when it came to minor matters. They also say he was a night owl, a bad singer, a bad dancer, and that he played at being a street tough, sitting with other hardboiled types. How many times did he break a beer stein with his teeth? How often did he crunch broken glass between his jaws, jaws descended from eight lieutenant generals? And how many times did he swallow that horrible mash, simply for the pleasure of titillating a gaggle of girls or shutting some fuckface's piehole?

The La Croix de Castries family had counted one or two archbishops, a marshal, an alliance with the Morte-marts, a Knight of the Order of Malta, and even the wife of a president of the Republic. Who can top that? Still, someone even nastier and more snobbish than Saint-Simon might sneer that it only dates back to 1469, to Guil-hem Lacroix, an ennobled usurer. Thanks to the insatiable curiosity of Pierre Burlats-Brun, author of *Héraldique & généalogie*, we can step even further down the social ladder, from Guilhem Lacroix to Jean Lacroix, who already sounds an off-note, then from Jean to Raymond and from Raymond to Johan Le Cros, *fishmonger*—which, given the pride of the Castries, is humorous, even touching in its humility.

The Castries family thus boasted a minister of the Navy, shovelfuls of dukes and marquises, and even until just recently they were sitting comfortably, in the person of Henri de Castries, in the Moroccan leather chair of the CEO of Axa, which is like a new archbishopric or another ministry of finance. Henri de Castries is a graduate of the top business school, Catholic, patron of the French Scouts. He's not an ideologue—a right-winger, to be sure, but he still feels comfortable frequenting his old socialist classmates. He's married to Anne Millin de Grandmaison, his cousin (small world). Number 7 on the archangelic list of highest-paid executives, between Pinault and Mestrallet; as head of the above-mentioned corporation, he earned 950,000 euros in fixed income, in the name of the unnamable Father; 2,034,171 euros in variable income in the name of the sacrificed Son; and the rest (director's fees, stock options), in the name of the Holy Spirit, the smallest figure of the Trinity, 86,000 euros and change—almost a college professor's salary. Still, deep down, the Castries are just like us: they were mostly merchants, fishmongers, and their invisible family tree harbors hundreds of beggars and thousands of hunter-gatherers. But very often a sizable inheritance can be mistaken for destiny, and Marie Ferdinand de La Croix de Castries certainly saw it that way. Onward!

It's he who'll command the base at Dien Bien Phu, he's the one Navarre put in charge of the entrenched camp. Oh, he doesn't especially like it, does Marie Ferdinand de La Croix de Castries; he prefers wide-open spaces, wars of movement, the cavalry. But ultimately he accepts. And now here he is, in his shelter covered with mats and sacks of earth, in front of his a/c, riffling through imbecilic papers and gnawing on pencils. He sees the world through mosquito netting. Whatever happened to that cute little Spanish number he met last month? And what about the Viets, what do they do for R&R? He spits a shard of pencil into the ashtray, then decides to go for a walk. In the evening, Colonel de Castries dines with some officers. Then he returns to the command post. The moon hasn't yet risen. It's cold. He runs his palm over his close-cropped head. That evening, several purple tracers slash the hillsides; there's a sound of machine-gun bursts. The slightly disheveled colonel downs a second bottle. In the morning, fog chokes the valley. In his bunker, the colonel is bored.

Encircled

———

Slowly the camp was encircled. They hadn't seen it coming. On December 7, the Pavie Track was cut off. It became impossible to leave camp without suffering massive losses; for all around them was forest, jungle. And that was something Navarre hadn't counted on. From HQ in Hanoi, they don't have a clue! As for Marie Ferdinand de La Croix de Castries, who knows all about it, he seems to believe in a possible victory, he seems to believe (sucking on his cane or his measuring rod) that he's going to burst out of the ground from two meters below the surface and…—and what? He's not really sure, he hesitates…—and whip the herds of buffalo under the sun, pierce the gray skin of the rice paddies, tear down the bamboo arches! And yet, the troops sent out to reconnoiter barely make it past the camp limits. On the survey maps, arrows wander hither and yon, leap over rivers, fly over mountain passes; but here in Dien Bien Phu, they're pinned down. An arrow can easily cross over a hill at 1:25,000 scale, cross 1/25,000th of a stream, climb 1/25,000th of a mountain, and your hand can then plant a little paper flag on it. But at Dien Bien Phu, the little flags remain in their box, and the rivers are not 1/25,000th of themselves: they're actual size, and the hills are covered in betel palms and undergrowth, and what on Navarre's table over there is merely a centimeter, over here is twenty-five thousand times bigger! And after all, twenty-five thousand centimeters is two hundred fifty meters, and two hundred fifty meters of jungle, two hundred fifty meters of steep inclines, two hundred fifty meters intercut with cliffs, two hundred fifty meters of Vietminh, is not exactly the same as a centimeter of gridded paper. Instead of making maps at 1:25,000, the French general staff should make maps wider than the big wide world, on which rivers would be less fordable than real rivers and hills would be more uneven than real hills. For one might well have dropped 127 tons of bombs on Mercury Point, the supposed nerve center of the Vietminh's provisions: bicycles, pushed by former coolies wearing cheap canvas and sandals, immediately take to the roads, forging a whole network of new paths, despite the heavy sacks of rice and mortars on their backs.

———

Growing concerned, the last remaining Parisians go to see Navarre and visit the entrenched camp. They want to get an idea. Navarre meets them in Hanoi, in battle dress, holding a small rosewood baton. He has been accorded a visit by Mr. Jacquet, the secretary of state for foreign affairs. I'm not sure what Jacquet thought as Cogny listed the threats amassing around the entrenched camp; I don't know whether (as mayor of Barbizon) his pipe produced puffy white clouds like Corot's and Daubigny's; and no doubt he would have preferred even a third-tier restaurant to an officers' mess, and no doubt he didn't feel very at ease, standing between that hulking brute Cogny and the pinched, silent little Navarre. And then Jacquet goes to Dien Bien Phu, asks questions, doesn't seem very convinced. But by 4 p.m., it's time to leave, the Vietminh could attack at any minute. He's spent two and a half hours at Dien Bien Phu, not really enough time to form an opinion.

And so they send Mr. Pleven. Pleven has been, more or less, a minister nine times and Council president twice. He knows the score. Just before him, on February 7, Mr. de Chevigné, secretary of state for war, goes to Dien Bien Phu. On February 8, at a stopover in Nice, Pleven crosses paths with Jacquet on his way back to Paris. They swap impressions over coffee, and the impressions are not very good. Meanwhile, in Dien Bien Phu, what does de Chevigné see? A chamber pot. Yes. He sees that the garrison is living, *stricto sensu*, at the bottom of a chamber pot. And he sees that the Vietminh are occupying the entire rim of that pot. This is all most troubling. In a kind of demonstration, to entertain Chevigné, whose daughter has married a Castries and whose grandmother was the model for Proust's duchesse de Guermantes, the colonel has sent two battalions to attack the hills, supported by artillery and air cover. The point was to destroy a 75mm field gun that would sporadically fire on the camp. The two battalions of paratroopers were to scale Hill 781, backed by tanks and artillery. So what happened? Well, they barely managed to get over the rim of the chamber pot and advance a few kilometers, before, having sustained heavy fire, and despite the air support, they were forced to turn back.

On February 19, it was Defense Minister Pleven's turn to make an inspection. At around 11 a.m., he took off from the airfield in Hanoi, heading for Dien Bien Phu. Navarre didn't come, not wanting, he said, to influence the other man's judgment. Castries greeted him and described the military facility, the forces at his disposal.

Pleven, who had been in Indochina for ten days, was also wearing a curious battle dress, with legs that were too wide and pockets that were too large, in which he seemed to float. Crowning this was a panama hat, which in the jungles of Tonkin was a dubious accessory. Suddenly, turning toward General Fay, chief of staff for the Air Force, Pleven asked what he thought of the entrenched camp. "I would advise General Navarre to get out of Dien Bien Phu, or else he's done for," Fay replied without hesitation. For several minutes, the members of the small delegation stared fixedly at their shoes, and the visit ended on an awkward note. That evening, in the plane, Pleven seemed worried, chain-smoked. He left Indochina several days later—but not before presenting Navarre with the star of Grand Officer of the Legion of Honor. It's still unclear why.

Beatrice! Beatrice!

———

It seems that Dante, despite his medallion profile and his extraordinary adventures in the bowels of our woes, never, but never, glimpsed or knew or loved a girl named Beatrice, and that the great love he crooned over in book after book was just a literary artifice. Truly wicked tongues might add that he was in the habit of banging his domestics on the fly and that gentle Beatrice was in fact his servant, and that the old owl had sung her a vita nuova between two stacks of dirty dishes. And so, by one of those sentimental fervors that soldiers are prone to—a trait they share with poets—they baptized one of their strongholds "Beatrice."

A stronghold serves to protect the heart, to protect the heart of a military facility, a command post, or an airstrip against enemy fire. And, from stronghold to stronghold, a fortification secures the positions. As such, strongholds protect one another, like a band of close friends. In order to do this, so that the entrenched camp could be on cleared terrain where they could maneuver freely, they evicted the villagers, burned their houses, torched the copses and grapefruit trees. It was quite a bit of work, carried out by prisoners, or Arabs. Some thousand peasants had been displaced since the arrival of the expeditionary force. But now, Beatrice stands proudly amid her bouquet of bare spikes. At night, she's a ring of light surrounded by barbed wire, tunnels in the earth beneath wooden logs. A jeep with its windshield folded down on the hood navigates to the command post, then returns. Days go by. They wait. It's been weeks, months, that they've been waiting. It seems the Vietminh are going to attack. They dread it and long for it. Sometimes they forget about it.

March 13. Foul weather. At dawn, a Dakota lies grounded, in flames. Another one explodes near stronghold Isabelle. And from then on, everything falls apart. Another airplane catches fire. Two reporters, filming the scene, are hit by mortar fire; one dies, the other loses a leg. A little later, a fourth airplane catches fire. Another is shot down in mid-flight. They've been waiting for the confrontation, calling for it, and now here it is! And as usual, it's much less fun than in storybooks, much less pretty than in paintings, even sadder than in memories. It stinks of gasoline and dust. The air is full of smoke, you don't breathe so much as cough, talk so much as yell, sing so much as spit. Caught between the expeditionary corps and the Vietminh, the Thai villagers pack up and leave: it's the sign that an attack is imminent and the Vietminh have advised them to get out. It's strange to see those lines of men, women, children, and elders carrying what they can, slowly, inexorably, leaving behind their empty houses, as if real life has become just a stage set.

Suddenly, Christian Marie Ferdinand de La Croix de Castries thought he noticed something in the smoke from burning fuel, amid the first ruins. Yes, he did see it! There it was, and he didn't know if it meant victory or death. At that moment, there was a great "Oh!" in the entrenched camp. Everyone moved back. The colonel stood alone, right before the thing. He stopped and stared. Good Christ, what *is* that? It's not a tribe of Blacks, it's not a group of coolies bound together with wire, it's not the poor railway saboteurs he's heard about, it's not a single young man holding a Browning, no, it's a huge phantom rushing toward them. It's the People's Army.

The entrenched camp holds its breath. Based on aerial photos and informant intel, the attack is predicted for 1700 hours. The hour arrives under the great bloodless sky. Nothing happens. Five p.m. and one minute, two, five, ten...nothing. Still nothing. The legionnaires are silent, each man wrapped in his own anxiety, eyes wide open, breathing heavily, scraping the ground with his worn boot. Ten minutes! That's a damn long time, an eternity; the entire history of the world can be contained in ten minutes! Admiral Charnier comes up the Mekong with a flotilla of several gunships, in one minute. The emperor of Vietnam petitions for peace in two seconds, and one minute later the French are occupying Indochina. But they only occupy it briefly, for one minute after that, Ho Chi Minh arrives and proclaims independence. Then it's war, for a minute, and here we are at the very final seconds of this great slice of life, at the Saturday evening of creation, an instant before sunset. Suddenly, at 5:30, an enormous tumult pulverizes the silence. These are not merely a few harassing volleys, they're a hammer blow that splits your skull in two. Rows of men dash forward with noses to the ground, what a rude awakening! They quickly thread their way into the gutters, run in the dust, and from every direction it's hit and slash, cables are ripped out, ceilings piss earth, shelters collapse. In several instants, the entire facility of the entrenched camp is convulsed. It no longer looks like a well-behaved giant, standing in the middle of the jungle—that's over. From all sides, they wallow in rubble, the camp is pounded mercilessly. Every three seconds, the earth trembles and soil rains down. Beatrice no longer exists.

They say that that's when Marie Ferdinand de La Croix de Castries began showing signs of despondency and exhaustion. The Vietminh shells had opened in him an abyss of perplexity. For the next two months, Castries would not once leave his shelter. He wore his helmet night and day, and scrupulously relieved himself in the casque bearing his insignia.

Navarre Up Close

―――

While the battle is turning disastrous, Mme Navarre, in Paris, flits from salon to salon, conversing herself hoarse. She toasts her rangers only with the best Chambertin, tickles her palate with fine liqueurs, riddles partridge wings with small holes, and shivers at the crackle of a meringue. She is invited everywhere; her only enemies are the lemon slices concealed in bouquets of shrimp. From Saigon, General Navarre is preparing his Operation Atlante, which involves advancing, by a piston effect, from south to north, so as to conquer a large portion of the territory. But Operation Atlante goes awry; and the more Navarre dreams of his grand strategic movement toward the upper mountain plateaus, the farther he drifts from the verdigris clay valley of Dien Bien Phu.

In the evening, after watching a movie at the Eden, Navarre goes home, climbs the stairs, pulls on his nightshirt and slippers, returns to his work table, and dreams. He dreams for a moment of writing that note he's quietly been pondering for quite some time, a short scholarly note about the childhood of Antoine Henri de Jomini, the genius, the greatest military strategist of the nineteenth century—"Napoleon's soothsayer," they used to call him at the war college. And since the nights are long, he rereads a bit of the book by Courville, the great man's great-grandson; it reeks of panegyric, but he adores that. Then he imagines what his essay would be like, a brief note on Jomini's childhood in the alleyways of Payerne, like a more erudite *War of the Buttons*, larded with maxims by the master and illustrated with trash can barricades on strategic street corners. But a dull anxiety pervades him. Has he indeed followed Jomini's precepts at Dien Bien Phu? Did he truly absorb the master's lessons at the war college? Has he let others lead him onto a slippery slope? Seized by doubt, he picks up *The Art of War* and plunges back into that tedious tome, barely disturbed by the noise of the air conditioner. Time passes, 1 o'clock, then 2 in the morning; and imagine his surprise to discover, the more he reads the celebrated score, that he had heard an entirely different melody. He suddenly feels troubled, feverish, riffs through the book faster and faster, and is forced to admit the extent to which his entrenched camp, his weird creation, contravenes not just one or two of Jomini's precepts, but all of them!

"According to my view," writes Jomini, "the real and principal use of intrenched camps is always to afford, if necessary, a temporary refuge for an army, or the means of debouching offensively upon a decisive point...To bury an army in such a camp, to expose it to the danger of being outflanked and cut off...would be folly." Goddammit to hell! he says to himself, what the fuck have I done! Indeed, Dien Bien Phu is neither a temporary refuge nor an offensive means, but a good way to bury his army on the spot, plain and simple. He nervously leafs through the pages of the book: "Despite all this, these intrenched camps," Jomini adds, driving the nail home, "when only intended to afford a temporary foothold..." Shit! Shit! Shit! What the hell is Jomini up to, he's making an ass of me, he's out of his mind! And a bit further on: "but it will never be more than a temporary refuge..." Great God Almighty, how had he never spotted that? And General Ely, and good old Marshal Juin, why hadn't they cried out: "Hold on, there, go back to your Jomini!"

He pours himself a scotch. What rotten luck that nobody in the entire French Army had read Jomini last year! He thought about General Fay, chief of staff of the Air Force: hadn't he clearly voiced his disagreement? Navarre brushes away the memory with a swipe of his hand. Nobody reads Jomini anymore, he muses...except, perhaps...and it's then that he notices in the distance, under a palm shank, behind a tangle of brush like an awful gnarl, like an enigma: two eyes. Then, his vision growing sharper: the face of the Vietminh general, Vo Nguyen Giap. Ah, yes!—*that* one has surely read Jomini, as well as Vauban and all his theories about sieges. We might have made a big mistake teaching those Vietnamese how to read, and in our language to boot!

Navarre then tries to lift his spirits. He parades before him all the great battles of History, all the entrenched camps: Didn't Bunzelwitz save Frederick II? Of course it did! Frederick the Great's stroke of strategic genius, no doubt about it! Hadn't he entrenched several hillocks behind piles of rubble, trous-de-loup, trapdoors, fences, fougasses? And the one at Mainz, didn't it prevent the siege of the town, had the French Army been able to launch one? And Wurmser's famous camp, didn't it extend the resistance in Mantua by two months?

But in Bunzelwitz, Navarre then thinks, in a final burst of pessimism, Frederick benefited from his adversaries' indecision. And in Mainz, they had to abandon the camp. And in Mantua, didn't the Austrian Army ultimately get wiped out?

The Diplomats

———

O n April 21, 1954, while the French expeditionary force
was at death's door, the American secretary of state,
John Foster Dulles, made a quick stopover in France.
Several days later, Dulles and Foreign Minister Georges
Bidault were at Quai d'Orsay for a small reception.
Here they are, seated side by side on a sofa, before a lac-
quered table, posing for *Paris Match*. Their hands mimic
a weighty conversation; Dulles seems to be saying to Bidault, "Surely you agree with at least the main points of
my argument?" while Bidault, with a quizzical but con-
ciliatory pout, stares at the window. The atmosphere is
relaxed, the two men know and seem to like each other.

We don't know whether Bidault mentioned Bergson,
whom Dulles admired, and whom, as a young man, he'd
studied under during the year he squandered in Paris.
But we do know that it was during a second pause, which
they executed in the company of two or three secretaries
of the Quai, that Dulles, unexpectedly moving aside and

bending at a strange angle, with convoluted hyperbole and looking as weaselly as could be, turned suddenly toward Bidault:

"And what if I gave you two?" he blurted.

"Two what?" asked the French minister, taken aback, unable to make the connection between the diplomatic and rather banal conversation they'd been having about Dien Bien Phu, and this question with its absurd phrasing.

"Two atomic bombs," the secretary of state specified.

Several moments later, Maurice Schumann sees a pale Bidault enter his office. He's mildly surprised, as Bidault is normally punctilious about etiquette, and as minister he has always demanded a strict adherence to protocol. But on that day, Bidault barges in without knocking, stumbles over the rug as he crosses the room, sits in the plain chair facing his secretary of state, and stammers: "Do you know what Dulles just said to me?" Schumann looks at him, perplexed. "He offered me two atomic bombs to save Dien Bien Phu."

John Foster Dulles had spent a year in Paris in his wild youth. He had frequented the high society of the Belle

Epoque. But all those Marie Brizards hadn't gone to his head, and during that idyllic Parisian sojourn, neither strolls in the Luxembourg Gardens nor the café tables of Montparnasse had made him forget his career prospects. For Dulles was not just some crazy young student, a vague denizen of the Latin Quarter, but an institution: *the Dulleses*. Brother of the director of the CIA, but also grandson and nephew of the thirty-second and forty-second secretaries of state of the USA. They even left *their* name on an airport in the nation's capital, Washington-Dulles, which links them with America's founding father.

It is thus a veritable establishment who leans toward Georges Bidault that April day. Next to him, Bidault is just a minor enterprise; his father was an insurance broker in Moulins, and all he has around him is a forest of rural landowners, Catholic and small-minded. Whereas Dulles is a veritable multinational. And amid the remnants of the past, across miles of news flashes and newsprint, we can spot quite a few corpses in his wake.

The previous year, he and his brother had masterminded the fall of Iranian Prime Minister Mossadegh, who had conceived the unfortunate notion of nationalizing the oil industry. The Anglo-Iranian Oil Company felt swindled. So Allen Dulles freed up a million dollars to topple Mossadegh, thereby blocking democratic reforms in Iran for a very long time. And you have to read the CIA's mission orders, its extraordinary laconicism, to grasp just what kind of operation was involved: *Target—Prime Minister Mossadeq and his government. Objectives—Through legal, or quasi-legal, methods to effect the fall of the Mossadeq government; and to replace it with a pro-Western government under the Shah's leadership.* But even as he's speaking with Bidault, John Foster Dulles is responsible for a whole other operation, the ouster of President Jacobo Arbenz Guzmán of Guatemala, who was envisioning an agrarian reform that would distribute ninety thousand hectares of land to his country's neediest peasants. This endangered the interests of the American multinational United Fruit Company, which rejected the buying price of three dollars per acre that it had nonetheless declared to the IRS, undervaluing its landholdings to lower its taxes. United Fruit, hoist with its own petard, had reached out to the Dulles brothers, who owned the most prominent law firm on Wall Street and were, moreover, major shareholders in United Fruit. The Dulleses engineered a tailor-made coup that delivered the country to a military junta, and Guatemala plunged into a long period of violence that left hundreds of thousands dead.

We find them again seven years later, on January 17, 1961, the apex of our sorrows, in Elisabethville, State of Katanga—for their characteristic blend of amiability and villainy spared no continent. On that day, at 4:50 p.m., an Air Congo DC-4, number 00-CBI, touched down from Moanda. Three men, roped together, were pushed roughly from the plane and bundled into a jeep. The sinister procession headed toward the residence of a Belgian settler. Among the three prisoners was Patrice Lumumba, the first prime minister of the Republic of Congo, which had only recently gained its independence. At 5:20, the jeep came to a halt. Lumumba and his two comrades were thrown to the ground, dragged into the house, and tortured. Three hours later, the convoy started up again. A long half hour of driving, then they stopped in Mwadingusha. The Belgian police commissioner Frans Verscheure made the three prisoners get out of the car. And while they're pushing him to the edge of the shallow ditch where he will be executed, let us focus for a moment on Lumumba himself—and let us see, via the flagrant contrast between him and the other man, who *Dulles* was, what Dulles *didn't want*, from which we can divine the world he fantasized and tried to construct with his thicket of intrigues. But first, we have to go back in time and see Patrice Lumumba as a child, a farmer's son from a small village; see his gentle, shy, but determined smile, his serious face, the Protestant school where he droned out the rudiments of catechism, his fervent readings as an autodidact, the life of a laborer that he escaped by plunging desperately into books. Then let's look at him again sometime later, as an office employee in a mining company. He comes to understand the fundamental importance of raw materials, and he notes how the Congolese executives are excluded from power. These two revelations stick with him, and they are still with him, at 5-something p.m., between two bouts of torture.

In early July 1960, barely two weeks after the Congo had become independent, the Belgians staged a military intervention to make Katanga and its mineral resources the nucleus of a new Congo, sans Lumumba. They plotted to remove the prime minister from office. On August 18, the National Security Council of the United States expressed concern over the Congolese situation. And that's when *the Dulles boys* stepped in. Lumumba constituted a serious threat to American interests; CIA director Allen Dulles concluded that he must be gotten rid of "by any means."

This is why it's no exaggeration to say that five months later, on January 17, 1961, when Lumumba was seized by his torturers for the final time, before being brutally murdered in the jungle and his body dissolved in an acid bath, *the Dulleses* were there, amid the invisible spectral forces that accompanied the farmer's son with the gentle smile and serious face, in those final moments when he no doubt realized, with a horrifying mix of sadness and disgust, how right he had been to plunge into books, to fight with such determination, which now left him victorious and yet defeated, assassinated, because *their* violence and determination were so much larger; when he realized how badly he had underestimated the viciousness with which they would preserve their power. And as those specters accompanied him, the man who had led a victorious resistance and expelled the Belgians from the Congo saw that, although this was certainly something, in a sense it was still nothing, the Belgians were nothing: the real power—and he'd known it all along, ever since he'd been an office employee for a mining company in South Kivu—was the Union Minière du Haut-Katanga. And if the human spirit has its abysses, where the administrators of the Union Minière congregate; if no one has ever penetrated its deep layers, the Earth's crust as thick as our skulls and hermetic as language, where they drill down four kilometers to find gold, copper, and other ores; where you can fall to the bottom of the pit you've dug at a rate of sixteen meters a second before hitting the mine face; where you can suffocate in the atrocious heat; where some manage to sneak in, looking to scrape out a few nuggets and get back up with their meager loot in order to live a better life, but the mining police are vigilant, and when they think they've spotted one, they cut off the tunnel's air supply and asphyxiate him;

while outside, the mines form vast cities, heaps of iron surrounded by slag; and in that State of Katanga, where they've extracted so much cobalt and copper that it must represent a major portion of the metals currently in circulation around the globe, ten-year-old children labor, perish in tunnel collapses, smother, drown—and so it was that the dazed Lumumba, flanked by Belgian militiamen and still in shock from the torture he had undergone, dove deeply into himself, into the fissures of the human soul and, between those burning partitions as between the partitions of a mine, thought he saw a minuscule, bacterial population, deaf and blind but voracious, little beasts that had left the planet surface at the dawn of time and come to live here in the heart of darkness, but unfortunately for them a predator had followed them down, a tiny worm, a miniature monster whose hideous mouth is a vulva ringed with suction cups. But all that depth is nothing, he tells himself, and even the deepest drilling, almost thirteen kilometers below the surface, is nothing: they'd have to penetrate far past the crust where speleologists whimper, far past the mantle, down to the core, a dense mass of fused metal made molten by convection, and even then you'd merely graze against—not Hell, which is not very deep—but that which provides the Earth's magnetic shield and allows us to set our compasses and voyage across the oceans and appropriate the planet. But if we really want to know horror, Lu-mumba thinks to himself with a start, that's not where we should look, not at the abysses, the living creatures, the insane drilling, not even the human soul: no, if we really want to be horrified, we'd have to creep into the office where Eisenhower and Dulles are talking and hide under the carpet, so as to hear what's said behind closed doors, overhear the Dulles brothers talking informally, hear them speaking freely; for it's there, in that ethereal, temperature-controlled, immunized, otherworldly space, where note-taking is prohibited as if everything, apart from the scrupulous transfer of their dividends, should be erased from History; it's there, between the thick mortadella sandwiches that Dulles adored and the glass of Schweppes that a smiling secretary sets down, between a polite thank-you and a quick phone call to a colleague, between the mechanical filing of a document and a frank exchange on American interests in Africa, that they pondered something of which McCarthyism was but the unpolished media face, that they skillfully orchestrated the Cold War mechanism that led the world to the brink of Chaos. And as the line of condemned men reaches the top of the steep path, and the first prisoner slowly walks down toward the field, flanked by mercenaries, someone puts a hand on his shoulder and whispers in his ear: "Don't worry, you won't feel a thing." Suddenly, the prisoner's entire being stiffens and he begins to scream, is quickly gagged, tied up, blindfolded, shoved against a tree, while the other repeats with a snicker, "Don't worry, you won't feel a thing." There is a burst of gunfire and a militiaman saunters across the field, leans over the body, and nods; then they hose everything down, drag the body to a pit, and it all happens a second time, a second time that the frail silhouette appears at the top of the steep path, a second time that the condemned man lets out a sob, and a second time that they drag his corpse aside. But the third time, when they order Patrice Lumumba to walk to the middle of the field, he says to himself, "I'm going to look death in the face"; and so, when the executioners try to blindfold him, something in him goes rigid and he refuses; his silhouette so weightless on that early morning, looking so young, the ebony trees, the light, that acid taste in his mouth! On a famous photograph, taken during the negotiations five months before independence, Lumumba smiles; at thirty-five, he will soon be prime minister, for only two months and twenty-one days. His face is relaxed, but his eyes, alongside the youth, determination, and gentleness, betray a glimmer of distrust, a reserve, perhaps a certain shyness; and there is an insane complicity between his determined gaze, his black skin, his unfathomable youth, and the sordid circumstances of his death. It's as if that photo had been taken the instant before his death, and he was brazenly throwing his youth in our faces. We are suddenly with him in the field, between the tree riddled with bullet holes and the thugs, and the passage of time makes no difference, the ebony trees and the odors of night make no difference, the steep path makes no difference. Alone amid the soldiers, Lumumba staunchly refuses to be blindfolded. He demands to look death in the face. There is a scuffle. They grab him and bind him tightly. He lets out a sob of anguish. He struggles some more, and while they grip him firmly and try to lash him to the tree, he feels an obscure desire. "Death in the face," he says to himself. And he closes his eyes.

Telegrams

═══

General Navarre's mind was in a million places, but up until April 21, there was one thing on which he stood firm: his adamant opposition to a cease-fire. And in the dozens of letters and telegrams he exchanged with the high command and members of government, he never stopped iterating and reiterating, in martial tones, what a disgrace and a mistake it would be to halt the fighting. His conviction was impressive.

But a few hours before Dulles's visit to Paris on April 21, Navarre woke up on the wrong side of the bed. News from the entrenched camp was miserable, his horoscope even worse, the weather rotten. What have I done? he wondered, sad and discouraged after a sleepless night. It was then that he sent General Ely his historic missive. Barely a week before the fall of Dien Bien Phu, hardly a few days before the war was definitively lost, between two bouts of anxiety, General Navarre abruptly changed strategy. Only idiots never change their minds, he mused. Sitting at his Mazarin desk, staring at the marquetry and sucking on his blotter, he wrote: "After due consideration"—leaving out his matinal malaise—"I now believe that an immediate cease-fire would be preferable to negotiations."

This abrupt, unequivocal reversal, the authoritative tone buttressing a viewpoint that was diametrically opposed to the one he'd upheld intransigently for months, deeply shook the joint chiefs. "What did this sudden about-face mean?" wondered General Ely. "How can we interpret it?" The question, like so many others—dinosaurs' extinction, missing link, iron mask—went unanswered.

The best soap operas pick up at each new episode. And so, in early May, another telegram. Navarre now gauges that "*if* Dien Bien Phu were to fall, an immediate cease-fire without prior negotiations would be impossible." General Ely is dumbfounded. Navarre is sounding the retreat, changing his mind at the drop of a hat. On May 5, still another telegram. This time, a cease-fire can only be reached *on condition of iron-clad guarantees for the future.* And yet, on the questionnaire written by the French delegation in Geneva, to the question "Who would benefit from a cease-fire?" Navarre answered without hesitation: "The Vietminh."

It's painful to read these telegrams, like being confronted with a rare combination of purposefulness and bewilderment; the tone is cold and haughty, but the content is weak, ill-assured. Navarre is in over his head. We can imagine the poor general, lost in some far corner of the world, well aware that his career is going down in flames, padding about pale and haggard in the hallways of the sumptuous residence he felt entitled to demand, in the time of his greatness only a few months ago.

But here's the thing! His obsessive fears and inner turmoil don't merely poison the atmosphere in Hanoi or Saigon but rapidly infect the entire French government; and during the first week of May, his doubts contaminate even the highest ranks. Everyone in France is divided, every person *of authority*, soldier, politician, expert of every stripe. On one side, the partisans of an immediate cease-fire; on the other, those of a negotiated cease-fire. It's a numbskull version of the Dreyfus Affair, a Panama for cretins. At a time when the war is already lost, everyone rips everyone else's eyes out; even the sacrosanct War Council is violently split. The famous telegram from early May enflames even the coldest, most seasoned hearts; they tear out what little hair they have left. Navarre is contagious. Everyone goes berserk. They biff each other at High Command, kick each other at the Council of Ministers, scratch and bite in the back rooms. You have to choose sides. You shout "immediate cease-fire" or "negotiated cease-fire," and no quarter!

———

ONCE THE ENTRENCHED camp fell, the humiliation was unbearable; Navarre suffered violent bouts of anxiety and stopped going outside. The muffled condescension of his peers hurt him worse than outright disdain. He was mortified. Dreading the weakness he felt, which actually might have made him more approachable, more human, he professed an ever greater firmness and became even more sectarian and retrograde. He lived in a state of obdurate resentment. And never again would he see as clearly as he had for a few moments in May, at the cost of a brief suspension of his faculties and accompanied by great suffering, when his career was obliterated and his whole life lost its meaning, and he, the standard-bearer of victory, he whose *cerebral machinery* (they said) *was admirable for its precision*, had been beaten by those people he thoroughly despised, those *Annamite peasants*.

He'd had a brief epiphany, fifteen minutes before the fall. In his vast residence—this Indochinese governors' palace that, several months earlier and full of himself, he had shamelessly requisitioned—strolling after nightfall near the carp pond (built according to the pharaonic demands of Paul Doumer), wandering among the thirteen hectares of park with his orderly discreetly trailing behind, plodding toward a light that he couldn't see, perhaps Navarre momentarily learned something from the vertigo of such a defeat. All day long he had paced back and forth, ceaselessly covering the hundred square meters of his lavish office, which grew smaller and narrower the more he trod around it. His anguish dug invisible channels in the carpet, his eyes were drawn to the lacquer folding screen given him by Bao Dai, with its dark patches and pale shadows, before which he halted, speechless, as if before the thick black waters of a pond, facing that weighty darkness in which minuscule gold leaves sparkled. Then still more feverishly he had crisscrossed the miles of corridors in his residence, anxiously penetrating into dozens of ceremonial rooms, empty in the late afternoon, seeking, among the thirteen hundred square meters of the palace, someone or something: he wasn't sure what.

He walked and walked in febrile anxiety, felt like he was falling. Now, as he passed through the alley of mango trees, their thick shady leaves already plunged in darkness with the fading of daylight, it no doubt occurred to him that his career was finished, that it would end on a horrible note, a disaster, a bloodbath. From afar, he noticed the neoclassical façade with its off-putting austerity, and the superiority emanating from the edifice wounded him, like a denial of his very person. "I should have listened to my father and become a teacher," he said to himself. But the cliché was no comfort; if anything, it made him feel worse. He saw himself as a boy studying his lessons; his whole childhood paraded before him and struck him as dull. His cold discernment no longer helped. And suddenly, he thought he heard a cannon blast. He jumped. The battle was almost over, he thought, as if he could hear Dien Bien Phu all the way from Hanoi, from the peaceful palace garden in which he'd be the last tenant.

But he'd heard nothing. Nothing more than insects smacking against the lamppost, which shattered his eardrums like the screech of a steam whistle. He stopped up his ears. He was exhausted and advanced with slow steps, so slow you could barely see him moving in the dark; and by the time he finally, painstakingly reached the bower, he had aged. He sat absently on a fragile gilded chair; a servant stood at a distance. His orderly pretended to keep walking. He thought he was alone. Night fell. He didn't move. "The closer one gets to power," he mused, "the less responsible one feels." He didn't remember where he'd heard that, and it started buzzing around in his brain, around the little lamppost called conscience. "The closer one gets to power, the less responsible one feels." His gaze became lost in the night, looking toward the park, in the direction of trees darker and thicker than night. "They said something about twenty thousand casualties," he thought. Each word seemed to be looking for something inside him. Twenty thousand casualties. Navarre tried to imagine what that meant, the lives of twenty thousand men. And he couldn't. "And the North Africans, the Annamites," he thought, and it plunged him into a kind of perplexity, a confusion. "North Africans…Annamites…"—were they counted among the twenty thousand dead since the beginning of the war? "They talked about fifteen thousand North Africans, yes, fifteen thousand, and forty-five thousand Indochinese, it's true." He tried to count, tried again, but the numbers scattered. Night had fallen. Navarre was alone. Alone with his eighty thousand corpses.

All that remained was Navarre's inner self, a void. But the void spoke. It spoke about the dead, all by itself, and an unfamiliar sadness came over him. "And the Vietminh?" he suddenly thought, without quite knowing what he meant, "and the Vietminh, how many dead, how many?" Then he remembered a note he'd been handed in Paris, when he assumed his functions, at the meeting of the joint chiefs. It was in a file in which losses were tallied. He vaguely remembered a column, his eyes slowly rose up the line of ink, and he saw: five hundred thousand soldiers. And in another column: one hundred thousand civilians. "Six times more than us," he thought. His hands clutched the wicker armrests, his nails dug into the gilding. He thought he was dying.

Yes, perhaps that evening, before the dark alley of mango trees that Doumer had planted, in the heady silence of his conscience, Navarre considered dying. "How is this possible?" he cried out. His cry did not pierce the darkness. "How can a modern army lose to…to…" He couldn't find the words. "To an army of peasants!" he grumbled. But already he didn't believe it. His servant came toward him, asked what he desired, and Navarre realized he'd been talking to himself. "Nothing, thank you, Minh, no need to stay, go home." The boy vanished.

He watched the Vietnamese servant move away, a small brown stain on the palace façade. By now, you could barely distinguish the trees from the night. Navarre was in darkness. He remained there, silent, petrified. The war was lost. Up until then, he had had a brilliant service record, had done everything his parents wanted, had shown himself to be obedient, respectful, a good pupil. And he had wanted to become a soldier, maintain the honor of his country, his empire. It was all fucked. In one shot, because of this goddam war, he was going to have to carry this bitterest of defeats: wasn't he the very first to lose against wogs, yellow men? "What have we done?" he thought. "What have I done? I don't know."

But actually, this time, he did know. It lasted one minute. For one minute, he stopped thinking like an officer educated at Saint-Cyr, like a captain relentlessly pursuing the pacification of Morocco, and for a brief moment he saw that all his usual rhetoric—honor, country—was a trap. "I'm going crazy," he muttered. When suddenly, through the heavy mango branches, he thought he heard a cry. He stood up and walked into the shadows, hands in front of him, frantic. He called out, "Where are you? Where are you?" His foot struck against a tree root, and it was as if a sword had sliced through his entrails; he dropped his riding crop, stumbled forward in the dark. "I've lost everything!"

But he hadn't lost a thing. It was the hundreds of thousands of coolies laboring in the mines or plantations who had lost something, not he; it was the Vietnamese People's Army that had lost five hundred thousand men, the occupied country that had been ravaged and wounded. Navarre had merely blown a career, and by his own doing. His entire life, he had persevered in his ideas of order and honor, in the conviction of his superiority;

despite all signs to the contrary, he had stubbornly clung to his rigid, blinkered conceptions. And up until then, he had reaped many narcissistic and material benefits from them. His entourage profited handsomely from his narrow view of the world; in the French Empire, his status as officer conferred practically limitless privilege. And the neo-Renaissance architecture, at once grandiose and vulgar, of the Indochinese governors' palace bore witness to the astronomical power of his egotism.

Didn't they call Navarre *one of the purest examples of Western militarism*? But now, all that was finished. His military life was over, ending in total defeat. He had just shot off a series of nonsensical telegrams, and life suddenly seemed absurd. He considered suicide. But he didn't do it. And gradually, as he reached the short gravel walkway leading to the palace steps, his spirits lifted. Gradually, he could again learn dispassionately, or pretend to learn dispassionately, from his defeat. Gradually, as he inched forward toward the light from the lampposts that dotted the hideous palace façade, he left the Vietnamese corpses to pile up in the lanes of boxwoods; he even thought he saw the bodies of his own soldiers, and they meant nothing to him. Gradually he abandoned the coolies and their slave labors to the darkness, their suffering was swallowed by the night, and by the time he reached the front porch and his domestics opened the heavy doors for him, he had forgotten all of it. In the foyer, his eyes lingered on the huge world map that showed the now obsolete borders of the French Empire. "The world is tiny," he thought. Then, with a firm step, he attacked the first tread of the master staircase—and nearly skidded.

The Partisans

═══

It's May Day. In the Tuileries Gardens, a girl is selling sprigs of lily of the valley. In Geneva, where peace negotiations are under way while the war still rages, people are strolling in the parks. But in Dien Bien Phu, it's over. You shit wherever you can, in the tunnels, off the edge of trenches, and roll the dead as far away as possible. On May 3, the last volunteer paratroopers report to the command post. They get a kiss on both cheeks and a paratrooper insignia pinned to their chest. Good work. On the 4th, the attacks resume. On the 5th, the Vietminh are practically at Isabelle. On the 6th, the eastern peaks are lost, and the remnants of battalions cling to the reverse slopes. They have only two days of provisions left and Castries is down to his last bottle of cognac.

At around 3 p.m., the French see from afar the Vietminh's political functionaries start to dance. They dance, sing, shout for joy. Most of them are children. It's like a grass fire. The foliage is bathed in light. But late that afternoon, it starts up again. Artillery pummels the remains of the entrenched camp. Darkness falls. People are dying on all sides. They retreat from foxhole to foxhole, stack up corpses for protection, and flit among them like sparrows in a hedge.

In the morning, small men dressed in cheap green canvas, wearing sandals made from rubber tires, reach the crests. They are coolies from the Michelin plantations, miners from Ninh Binh, Annamite peasants. Now they're holding machine guns and stepping over the dead. There is debris everywhere, pulverized bunkers, scraps of wood, barbed wire. It all lies inert in the viscous mud, like after a storm. And the great battle that promised a horrible end concludes like a polo match. Soldiers line up. The Vietnamese enter the shelters, holding their noses. They discover piles of corpses and carpets of shit. The final telephone call between Cogny and Castries included no cry of "Long live France!" as legend has it; and despite an avalanche of denials, Castries did indeed hoist the white flag. Passerat even claims that when the Vietminh burst into the command post, he cried out, "Don't shoot me!"

The next day, May 8, in Paris, under the Arc de Tri-
omphe, they'll celebrate the end of the Second World
War. And on Saturday evening, in Hanoi, for practically
the last time, the nightclubs will be packed.

A Board Meeting

The first to arrive was Emile Minost, president of the Banque de l'Indochine. He fingered his short mustache, advancing with a determined step toward the spiral stairs leading to his office. He sat down, picked up a folder, leafed through it distractedly, then headed to the shareholders' meeting. The second one to cross the threshold of 96 Boulevard Haussmann was Jean Bonnin de la Bonninière de Beaumont, a firebrand. He had married a Rivaud de La Raffinière, sired three brats, and his modest tribe had thus solidly linked itself to the Rivaud Bank, whose prosperity derived from countless rubber plantations. The bride's brothers had gotten him elected a deputy of Cochinchina. In 1940, he had voted to give Pétain full powers, and at the Liberation he was briefly imprisoned because of dubious connections. After which, he abandoned politics for strictly business. He was CEO of two rubber conglomerates, the Société Financière des Caoutchoucs and the Compagnie des Caoutchoucs de

Padang, honorary president of the Rivaud Bank, then honorary president of the Plantations des Terres Rouges, the Société de Culture Bananière, and many others. But his main role consisted in cultivating useful friendships and organizing hunting parties and upper-class social gatherings.

In the corridor, he crossed paths with Minost, who was coming down to greet the bank's board of directors and who grimaced when he saw him, as he found the man's conspicuous dilettantism irritating. But as he was giving Jean de Beaumont a cold hello, after the other man's feeble civilities, François Marbeau came to rescue him. Marbeau was the bank's auditor, a man of the finest milieu. He had married his mother's grand-cousin, thereby marking his allegiance to the clan, all the more so in that she descended from a banking family in Boulogne-sur-Mer. As for his brother, he was director of the Sucreries Coloniales sugar refinery, and his father had been mayor of Meudon, a respectable career.

Imagine actors who never revert to being themselves but go on playing their parts in perpetuity. The curtain falls, but the applause doesn't snap them out of their role. Even when the auditorium is empty and the lights out, they never leave the boards. No use screaming at them that that's enough, we get it, we know the story by heart: they'll keep right on acting, treading and declaiming onstage. It's as if they've become engrossed in themselves, caught in their own game, hearts pierced by their own arrows. Their round dance would be both lovely and awful, poignant and absurd, and you wouldn't know whether to laugh or cry.

The board of directors took their seats around the large table. They shook hands, murmured a few words, dropping scraps of syllables onto the sand of decorum. A domestic served sparkling water. The representative from the Lazard Bank went to find his place. Minost obsequiously rushed over to greet him. They discussed the political situation, the tragedy in Indochina; David-Weill sat back down, and Minost went to greet his old friend François de Flers. Both men were former tax inspectors, and both devoted their lives to business. But Minost came from Provins and was the son of a law clerk. Flers was born in the eighth arrondissement of Paris, had served in Poincaré's cabinet at age twenty-four, and had become a deputy director at the Finance Ministry; he came in via the royal road.

There exists in Paris a sacred triangle, between the Bièvre River, the Parc Monceau, and Neuilly, where experts claim to have discovered a microclimate. Under the influence of the eco-landscaped structure of wide avenues, the gardens of private mansions, and the ideal exposure of vast café terraces and thanks to the lip of forest, the soft foliage of the Byzantine hazels, and the cool produced by the subtle white flowers of the pearlbush that, once withered, unfailingly scatter over lawns, the diurnal (and, to a lesser degree, nocturnal) hygrometric curves are apparently modified, thereby allowing a delicate fauna to grow and prosper happily. Existing far from the rubble of Belleville with its harsher climate, and very far from the deadly expanses of the capital's northern neighborhoods that spawn a robust but primitive population, this triangular zone forms an oasis, where the conjoined presence of fountain water and arborous shade has, from time immemorial, promoted the growth of a protected species: the future businessman.

The terms *intermarriage*, *relations*, *parentage*, *heredity*, and *lineage* should not be reserved for Amazonian primitives. The eighth and sixteenth arrondissements of Paris, in the heart of that sacred triangle, provide the opportunity for an in-depth study of what we would ordinarily call *family*. In the particular environment described above, singular customs have long been developed, which allow us to, if not challenge, then at least nuance the learned analyses of Claude Lévi-Strauss, by leaning on his alliance theory in intertribal marriage, so as to examine the ingenious play of combinations in the financial bourgeoisie, with its strong endogamic tendencies.

Thus, it was, above all, families that walked that morning into *96 Haussmann* in Paris. A parade of dynasties. The fundamental law established by the great ethnologist here finds its extreme and outsized illustration. Studies of the eighth arrondissement of Paris practically allow us to formulate a new alliance theory. Once the general relations between units have been extracted from large quantities of empirical data, and laws with predictive value isolated after a detailed monograph on the playground of the toniest lycée, we can in fact affirm, with only a razor-thin margin of error, that the elementary structures of kinship in the eighth arrondissement of Paris rest on eight terms: *brother*, *sister*, *father*, *mother*, *daughter*, *son*, *brother-in-law*, and *sister-in-law*, joined to one another with almost no negative correlation, such that, in each of the two generations in question, there remains a good reason to get married, either with the sister or brother of one's brother- or sister-in-law, as several Michelins have demonstrated, or else with a cousin (regardless if cross or parallel), the bourgeoisie being in matters of arranged marriages even more permissive than the Koran. This results in the simplest kinship structure imaginable, whereby everything—cars, houses, stocks, bonds, honorary titles, positions, annuities—remains inalterably in the family. Reduced to its essence, this elementary kinship structure of the eighth and sixteenth arrondissements in Paris is called, quite simply, incest.

In grave tones the board members evoked the lamentable defeat, *our* army, *our* dead soldiers. But they weren't there to moan, business must go on, and besides, hadn't the bank made all the necessary decisions, hadn't it been clairvoyant in divesting from its awkward Indochinese positions as early as 1947 and redeploying most of its activities elsewhere, far from the fighting, in other colonies? Obviously, the French Army had fought the best it could, and it had struggled, they reiterated, against an enemy that far outnumbered it. But at bottom, as everyone knew—as Minost knew, and had even announced just before "the Cao Bang disaster" five years earlier, before the five thousand dead—Indochina was already a mere blip in the bank's portfolio. They had discreetly liquidated their holdings, and the battles, all in all, had been over a colony that was already bled dry.

Minost was perfectly aware of this. Flers knew it too and had even known it for several generations, with a sure instinct that perhaps descended from the seventeenth century, from his ancestor Jean Ango, lord of La

Motte, secretary to the king, and counselor to the Parliament of Normandy. Charles Michel-Côte also knew it; as did Emmanuel Monick, who was board member or president of six or seven banks. All of them, sagely arranged around the conference table, looked at each other with staggering seriousness, exemplary gravity. Even the torture of having to listen to that idiot Jean de Beaumont bombard them for a solid minute with every possible cliché about the sacrifice of our soldiers and the greatness of France—he went so far as to evoke his distant kinship with Castries, he who would have chosen the slightest evening at the Jockey Club over any military ceremony—even that torment that his dilettantish buffooneries inflicted on them didn't make them flinch. Their patriotism was beyond reproach.

The porter pulled the door handle, and the members of the board were finally alone. Navigators of old fantasized about the great depths. They glided silently over smooth seas, made anxious by the great unknown void they imagined below them. They believed they discovered vestiges of it on the shore: sections of tentacles, shredded jellyfish, dry seaweed, the dead arm of a starfish. It was worry-making. And the room in which the board members were now enclosed to collect their dividends and decide the future was just as pale, diffuse, and obscure as the bottom of the ocean. Suddenly, the figures around Minost began floating like motes in sunlight. And it was as if one were seeing, not such and such a real bank, a precise and concrete incarnation, but *the* bank par excellence, the Idol.

It's just that the Banque de l'Indochine was not exactly your average bank. Like the Banque de France, it minted its own currency, which was legal tender in Indochina, in the Etablissements Français de l'Océanie in New Caledonia, in the Etablissements Français de l'Inde, and on the French coast of Somalia—in other words, around the world. The sum of its banknotes in circulation and of its current credit accounts was more than two billion. And every member of the board was not merely a technician, not just a successful financier or simple bank president. We find them in every domain: wood, gold, copper, cement, the Société Anonyme des Charbonnages in Tonkin, lighting in Shanghai, a rug factory. It's amazing: they know everything, do everything, administer everything. You buy an ice cream cone on Rue Paul-Bert in Saigon and don't realize that the company Brasserie & Glacières de l'Indochine has on its board the very wise Edouard de Laboulaye, representing the Bank. You change the tires on your Chevrolet and don't know that the rubber was produced by the Société des Caoutchoucs de l'Indochine, and that on *its* board sits Paul Baudouin, representing the Bank. You need water pipes for your house but are unaware that drinking water is distributed by the Compagnie des Eaux et d'Electricité de l'Indochine, on whose board presides Jean Maxime-Robert, representing the Bank. You strike a match, not knowing that it's sold by the Société Indochinoise Forestière et des Allumettes, whose board includes Jean Laurent, representing the Bank. You're on the Red River on your honeymoon, listening to a marvelous song performed by one of the famous zither players who, in Annam, beg for a living by the shore, and you sip your punch with no knowledge that the boat ferrying you belongs to a barging and towing company on whose board figures, yet again, a representative of the Bank. And if we were to continue the ludicrous inventory of companies that the Bank indirectly manages, we would also find housing loans, dredging, public works, and even a pawnbroker.

But this isn't limited to Indochina. Through its subsidiaries and holdings, the Bank's influence extends to saltworks in Djibouti, Sfax, and Madagascar, to tea plantations, stationery, phosphates, glassworks, and trolley lines. Miraculously, everyone at the Banque de l'Indochine seems to appear on other bank boards as well: one is also with the Comptoire National d'Escompte, another with the Messageries Fluviales, the Baron Georges Brincard is at Crédit Lyonnais, Joseph Deschamp at Crédit Industriel et Commercial (CIC), André Homberg at Société Générale—but no matter, it's clear that we're endlessly walking in the same footsteps, always knotting the same threads around the same puppets. This is not iron wire binding family wrists together, but golden strands linking and relinking the same names, the same interests; and we constantly run along the same nerves, the same muscle fibers, so that all the blood ultimately flows into the same heart. We could go on like this for hours, coming across the same people a hundred times over, on each board of trustees, in each private mansion, in each family tree, the way you could have come across the same rubber tree transplanted thousands of times in the plantation at Phu-rieng. We might well think that this would suffice for the entire colony, perhaps for all of France (since Crédit Lyonnais and the CIC are not colonial establishments, right?), and that all in all, since political power falls to just a few so as to keep democracy safe from the mercurial and often dubious will of Mr. Everyman, it would be better to clear the Palais Bourbon of the oysters, snails, and slugs who have taken up residence there for almost a century, and whose incompetence has pervaded society with the specious notion that the majority knows its interests better than a small group of duly qualified experts—experts who should in fact be in power by virtue of their experience, knowledge, and devotion to the public good. At bottom, this would be true democracy, the kind that François de Flers might be dreaming of as the board meeting gets under way, and that many financial authorities are surely dreaming of. It would keep political deliberations from interfering needlessly with decision-making. Because in the last analysis, as we're constantly told, laws are dictated by economics. So all you'd need is one meeting a year, at *96 Haussmann*, the headquarters of the Banque de l'Indochine, to candidly discuss problems and share out a few dividends. A board of trustees to run France!

———

NOW, at the climax of the drama, they sit around the table as usual. The servants have delicately relieved them of their coats. Minost lets his gaze drift through the window, where, among the dark branches of the plane trees, he momentarily discovers an outlet for his musings. Meanwhile, Michel-Côte drones on, comments on the tables, reciting vertiginous figures in monotones:

"The bank's share capital has risen to two billion francs, divided into four hundred thousand shares of five thousand francs each, fully paid and essentially registered."

A few throats clear. And Michel-Côte continues saying mass, finally reaching the crucial moment:

"Last year, the dividend paid out per share was three hundred and fifty francs. I'm pleased to report," he suddenly calls out, taking on a triumphal air that clashes with his smooth sales clerk face, "that this year it will increase to a thousand and one francs!" Despite their legendary decorum, there are a few audible clucks of satisfaction. It's true that this is quite a jump, the dividend having increased threefold. It is rigorously in proportion to the number of dead. In the shadow of France's defeat, after a widespread redeployment of the commercial bank's activities and holdings, this is a remarkable feat. It fully deserves some jubilation.

Flers and Beaumont exchanged a complicit glance, as if in the salon of the Greffulhes, whom Robert de Flers, his father and a friend of Marcel Proust, had so assiduously frequented. Charles-Valentin Dangelzer struggled to suppress a giggle. The situation was comical, even absurd. They won by losing, and oh, did they win! Minost sat with his head bent toward the table, lost in thought. He was listening. Perhaps at that instant he was exploring the innermost reaches of his conscience. Born in a poor provincial town with medieval ramparts, in the shadow of a notary's office, and not into luxury like Flers, no doubt he had hidden disabilities, perhaps a little pity, a wisp of remorse. Perhaps he glimpsed, in a moment of rapture, the corpses eaten by flies, the pulverized bunkers, all that inert flesh dredged in mud. He had been in the Resistance early on, active, diligent, a close associate of General de Gaulle, the indispensable financier of Free France, so how could he embrace this thing that he himself had orchestrated? How could he accept the dizzying gross of such questionable dividends without revulsion? And besides, he wondered, he, *the social climber*, the only one here who didn't owe his position to family ties or marriage, the one his colleagues secretly despised: hadn't they made him president of the bank at a critical moment, in order to erase the stain of collaboration, and to help them sell off their Indochinese interests? And in compensation for that fabulous ascent, wasn't it he who did the dirty work? He looked up pensively; and as Beaumont's piggy eyes squinted in gratitude, he felt a wave of disgust.

The Eye of the Hurricane

They filed out of the room in a cordial hubbub. Minost went last, shut his briefcase, bid good day to the usher closing down after him. Despite the excellent news he had announced, his mind was elsewhere, his gaze shifting left and right, from empty room to empty room, in the wan light of the offices. It was as if he was looking for someone or something, a souvenir. The hallway seemed endless. On the landing, he stopped before the bronze gladiator who for years had been dying on the window-sill, and there he had the stirrings of a bitter meditation on human life. But as if the deep currents of his being were suddenly obstructed, his thoughts turned to the en-trenched camp, defeat, death. At that moment, his suit felt constricting and he yanked on his tie. His valet had knotted it too tight.

Then, walking down the stairs, he recalled how the bank had quietly stopped investing in Indochina the minute the war started, rapidly divesting itself of its holdings and transferring its assets to more clement skies. And though he couldn't help feeling some bitterness, he had to admit that they definitely had a nose for this and they'd been so right to tiptoe out of there pronto.

When the rout of Cao Bang happened, the bank was already gone, and Indochina was just a husk, a semblance of a colony; he had calmly announced this at a trustees' meeting three months before that first defeat, three months before the five thousand dead. And now that the war was over, lost, the bank was in remarkably good health, its best year ever: 720 million in net profits, and dividends that had grown steadily throughout the war and would now triple. "Really incredible," Minost murmured as he waddled. And he fingered the fat black pearl spiking his tie and nervously twiddled his mustache.

As he exited *96 Haussmann*, a flock of pigeons took flight. Minost raised his eyes and gazed after them. It was beautiful. The car pulled up, he mindlessly took his seat in back, and his driver, turning around, handed him a tumbler of water. He drank it and felt better.

Boulevard Haussmann was experiencing one of its awful midday bottlenecks. Even here, people pounded on their horns. Good lord, what a ruckus! He thought about the weekend ahead, the tomato plants his gardener had transplanted on his instructions, and which had taken root; he had savvily picked a spot that was both sunny and damp. Suddenly, a poorly dressed housewife with a surly face yelled at his driver, who had almost hit her daughter; it's true that the little girl had nearly strayed from the crosswalk. Minost's attention was instantly drawn back to Indochina.

He thought about the war. Objectively speaking, he told himself in a sudden bout of guilty conscience, weren't they just monsters, every one of them, however distinguished they might be, however well brought-up and educated? Just monsters in elegant coats and sober gabardines, trench-coated monkeys? Didn't Flers already look like the monument he'd one day have at Père Lachaise, sober and flanked by stiff colonnades, but in the end, beneath the marble slab, just some leftover rot? And wasn't Beaumont a horrible baboon, with his smug, wonderstruck face and old-boy bonhomie? Did he really deserve the dividends he was receiving? How could they use words like *merit*, *work*, *ability*, *conscientiousness*, when crackpots like that could just show up and cash out with millions?

He leaned back, closed his eyes, and sighed. He heard the rumble of traffic, felt the car turn right, brake, then start up again. He opened his eyes. He was crossing the Seine, and he glanced at the gray waters. They weren't monsters, he told himself, it was their job that demanded these sacrifices. The bank's holdings represented a monstrous concentration of power, so what could you do? With a graceful motion, he smoothed his mustache, and the refinement of his person suddenly seemed to plead in his favor, like a moral equivalent. Hadn't he read the newspaper all these years, with those formidable articles by François Mauriac that routinely denounced the political crimes committed by France? Most of the bank's trustees were strict Catholics, but suddenly they stopped reading Mauriac, who had left *Le Figaro* for *L'Express* and declared his opposition to the war effort based on the very Catholicism they all practiced. Despite Mauriac's huge talent, despite his honesty in turning away from his political camp for the benefit of truth, which is perhaps the hardest sacrifice of all, once his intelligent and acerbic pen changed sides and bravely condemned torture, police violence, and the occupation of Indochina, they stopped reading him.

But even as the military had indeed practiced torture, bombed civilians, and jailed people arbitrarily; and even as members of parliament had advocated for war from the podium in grandiloquent tones, the bank's board members, for their part, had made no official statement. They had as usual remained on the sidelines, far from the fray, in the shadow of their offices, their rumpled raincoats thrown over a chair, solidly camped in front of their file folders. And of course, while the military were responsible for following iniquitous orders with such brutality, for constantly testing the limits of their authority, for acting randomly; and while politicians were guilty of promoting, against the people's interests, an ineffective and murderous war, and of lying about our intentions and our real chances of victory; while they idiotically celebrated "our soldiers" with such outrageous bad faith, when the ones who died were mainly the Arab, Vietnamese, or Black infantrymen who made up the bulk of our army; and while they constantly boosted the narrowest form of patriotism, using vulgar readymade expressions (as they still do today) to evoke the dead and employing a theatrical vocabulary that dishonors the very cause it claims to celebrate—while it was the military and the politicians who committed these heinous crimes, the gentlemen who had sat quietly around the conference table at *96 Haussmann* were guilty of far worse.

The car headed toward Sceaux, where Minost was to see some friends. And while it drove down Rue Saint-Jacques and skirted the walls of the Sorbonne, he resumed his painful little interior monologue. Yes, he said to himself, the bank was from the outset the perfect partner for the

French Army, it had a finger in everything that touched the financing and provisioning of the expeditionary force, and for six years it had found this a remarkable opportunity for enrichment. And thus the bank profited handsomely from the war that it fled, and whose end it lucidly predicted. But the pincer had two jaws. Even as the bank was siphoning investments out of the country, Minost suddenly thought while gazing at the sky, his eyes carried away by the gray turbulence, just as the bank was leaving Indochina, the war became its primary source of revenue. With parliament as its instrument and in the name of national honor, the bank's trustees furthered a murderous war from which they profited, even though they all knew it was lost. Behind Frédéric-Dupont's jingoistic kinetics, behind the colonial order defended by Viollette and Michelet, behind the enflamed patriotic declarations of de Lattre and Navarre, behind Bidault's procrastinations and Dulles's threats, the bank had patently wagered on France's defeat. While the French were just barely doing away with rationing coupons, and thousands of Vietnamese were suffering war and hunger on a daily basis, and the Vietminh troops were fighting with simple sandals on their feet, and some poor bastard was beating his drum to keep from weeping after not eating for two days, and for the feast of Tet they shared out a few slices of orange and some dry cakes at an improvised table, and the flame trees shed their red petals into empty cans, and fighter pilots hovered silently above the forest like giant birds, and grenade explosions churned up such a torrent of earth that men lost all sense of time—back in the accounting ledgers, the war had already been lost.

Lord, how far away the shackles were, how far the ragged coolies, how far the children working themselves to death, how far the cane blows, and how easy it was to be pragmatic and realistic thousands of kilometers away, to draw up a balance sheet and make projections, when you were in no personal danger of having to go on site to see what was happening up close. And the Flerses, the Hombergs, the Brincards, and that entire prodigious concentration of power that we call *a company*, the congenital absence of scruples that should make our skins crawl, could perfectly well sit there with manicured hands folded, nicely coifed and dressed in fine tailored garments, on the threshold. These are not people we're seeing, but functions; not intentions, talents, or knowledge, but the structure of the world. And we should look at all this at least once, full on, at the whole mass of interests, at the filaments binding them to one another in an enormous skein, a gigantic maw, a formidable heap of titles, properties, and numbers, like a formidable heap of corpses; we should stare for just one moment at the monstrous truth, the way they say that just before being swept away by a cyclone to your death, your face riddled by hail and stung by the wind, you would see the eye of the hurricane.

And yet, someone has to take responsibility, thought Minost, as if he were suddenly someone else. He felt a pang. After thirty years, he still hadn't managed to dissolve the totality of his remorse in the apprenticeship of good manners. And as the car skirted the walls of the property, he abruptly saw the entire mechanism of their enrichment, the bank's strategy; they had collegially decided which policy to follow and, in the interests of the institution and its shareholders, they had chosen the most lucrative path, and how could you blame them?

The car came to a halt under the arbor, the children approached shyly to welcome him. He picked up the hoop that a charming little girl in a pink dress had dropped on the lawn and told himself he'd managed everything smoothly, successfully. The bank had promoted the war and, without pointless scruples, had brought to fruition the collective mission it had been assigned: to shore up its holdings, increase its shares, balance its accounts, and most of all, come out on top and make as much money as possible. The little girl gave him a kiss; the hostess thanked him for the flowers that his driver had been thoughtful enough to buy and delicately pose on the back seat of the limo, handing them to him when they arrived so that he could offer them. And as he climbed the lovely porch steps, his gaze brushed over the stone garlands coiling around the vases, and he thought of something else. He had forgotten to tell himself that the logical end to this, a logic we all shared, one we had espoused alongside the privilege of being neither Vietnamese nor Algerian nor a worker—he had completely forgotten to tell himself that, in this game that aligned perfectly with the spirit of today's world, one must agree to speculate on everything, that nothing could be excluded a priori from the sphere of things, that only at this price could one amass wealth, and that on the unique and terrifying occasion of the war, he and the other members of the board had speculated on death.

The Fall of Saigon

───

All morning the helicopters had been circling above the embassy. It was chaos. In the city, everyone was taking something, piling up anything and everything, beds, fans, shades, mattresses. The police had started pillaging in turn, followed by the army. People ran through the streets, zigzagging among the scooters. The city was now surrounded by the Vietminh. The United States had followed in the wake of the French; the Frédéric-Duponts, Viollettes, Cabots, and Dulleses had dragged them into it; and the war that de Lattre swore before ten million television viewers would be over in two years, max, had lasted thirty. Thirty years. An entire generation had grown up under war, and another had spent its adulthood under war, its entire adulthood, and still another was born under war, had spent its entire childhood and youth under war. That makes for a lot of people. In thirty years, Vietnam received four million tons of bombs, more than all the bombs dropped by all the Allied forces during the

Second World War, on all fronts. And yet, Vietnam is
small, and that's a lot of bombs for such a small country.
In 1945, Ho Chi Minh had merely proclaimed its independence, even basing it on the French Declaration of
the Rights of Man; he hadn't declared war on anybody.

Soldiers run beneath the dark balconies, clutching machine guns; helicopters pass behind buildings. People go
up on rooftops, gesturing in panic. The roofs are full of
men and women hoping someone will take them away.
For the Vietminh are coming, and thirty years of warfare
has sharpened some hatreds, with plenty of time and opportunity for those hatreds to become almost a science.
The country is divided and reviled, and today an army
that has lived through thirty years of war is surrounding
Saigon.

Houses are aflame. Dead bodies litter the sidewalks.
A man runs, frantic. Shrieks. Women carrying children.
Fire. An odd mix of civilians and soldiers. People running in all directions. Scooters, bicycles, trucks, crowds
pulling trunks and bags. Faces tense and haggard. The
big American Chinook helicopters with their tandem
rotors, capable of transporting up to 150 people and
twelve tons of supplies, drag enormous bundles through
the sky. Saigon's nightclubs and brothels are closed. The

Blue Star is closed. The Baby Doll is closed. The Song Xanh, with its little stars on the ceiling, is closed. And now here come the young Vietcong soldiers with their choirboy faces. Here come the old Vietcong foxes, with faces like spiritual advisers.

On April 25, 1975, the Americans move out. Fans stop. Refrigerators stop. Cars break down. There are huge graveyards of refrigerators, necropolises of air conditioners, pyramids of dishwashers. Everything is dead. Then everyone rushes toward the last American boats, the last American helicopters, the last American airplanes—a horde. The pilots sort the passengers, gun in hand. In newsreels of the period, we can see through the windows crowds running after the planes, scooters and jeeps rolling desperately after them, as if after who knows what salvation. People cling to the wheels, to the flying ladder. They manage to haul up one or two by the skin of their backs.

Thousands of people launched on makeshift boats will die by drowning. How horrible, those boats overloaded with men, clusters of humans floating with the tides, those heaps of bodies, packages, bikes, screams, stupors. All those straw hats! A population is such a sad thing. It gets divided, cut off from itself; then time passes and it dreads being reunited, strangled in the pitiless net of out-side interests that have been imposed on it. O Kissinger, such a smarty-pants, they say, the Talleyrand of the Cold War, you sure look ridiculous with your relaxed smile, your know-it-all air, your famous glasses that let you see nothing. But never fear, the American colony has been evacuated, and the last Frenchmen are all gone. They were evacuated in silence; they snuck behind the curtain without attracting attention and got home. But toward the end, the retreat was pitiful. For the stragglers, it was more chaotic. There were people hanging in bunches to the undercarriages; and you could see the Italian ambas-sador himself clinging to the fence like a common thief. Ah, you should have seen the last Westerners evacuated in extremis, by helicopter, from the roof of the US em-bassy, during the fall of Saigon. You absolutely have to see the diplomats awkwardly climbing the rope ladders, neckties whipping in the wind. Bodies clinging to the rungs as their scarves sail off. What an atmosphere, like the end of the world; what a debacle! The pathetic hope of *an honorable exit* had consumed thirty years and mil-lions of dead, and this is how it all ends! Thirty years for such a farewell. Maybe dishonor would have been preferable.

Note

On the French and American side, there were a total of four hundred thousand casualties, counting artillerymen, Indochinese supplemental forces, and colonial troops who formed the bulk of our army. On the Vietnamese side, the war left at least three million six hundred thousand dead. Ten times more. As many as all the French and German casualties of the First World War.

Éric Vuillard is an award-winning author and filmmaker who has written ten books, including *Conquistadors* (winner of the 2010 Prix Ignatius J. Reilly), and *La bataille d'Occident* and *Congo* (both of which received the 2012 Prix Franz-Hessel and the 2013 Prix Valery-Larbaud). He won the 2017 Goncourt Prize, France's most prestigious literary prize, for *The Order of the Day* (Other Press, 2018) and was a finalist for the International Booker Prize for *The War of the Poor* (Other Press, 2020). Born in Lyon in 1968, he now lives in Rennes, France.

Mark Polizzotti has translated more than fifty books from the French, including works by Gustave Flaubert, Patrick Modiano, Marguerite Duras, André Breton, and Arthur Rimbaud. His translation of *Kibogo* by Scholastique Mukasonga was short-listed for the National Book Award in 2022, and his translation of Éric Vuillard's *The War of the Poor* was short-listed for the International Booker Prize in 2021. A Chevalier of the Ordre des Arts et des Lettres and the recipient of a 2016 American Academy of Arts & Letters Award for Literature, he is the author of eleven books.